THE TASTE OF
CHINA

Frederic Lebain   Jean-Paul Paireault

GALLERY BOOKS
An Imprint of W. H. Smith Publishers Inc.
112 Madison Avenue
New York City 10016

Compiled by Frédéric Lebain and Jean-Paul Paireault
Photographed by Jean-Paul Paireault
Designed by Sally Strugnell and Alison Jewell
Adapted and Translated by Lynn Jennings-Collombet

Acknowledgements

The publishers would like to thank the following for their
valuable assistance and cooperation in the production of
this book:

Madame Bayle, at Mas Le Plan in Lourmarin, for facilities for
location photography.
The shopkeepers of Lourmarin and Pertuis for their special
efforts to obtain and provide a variety of fresh and attractive
fish, meats and general provisions.
Morcrette, and Villeroy and Boch for the loan of glassware
and plates.
Cine Photo Provence, in Aix-en-Provence for film processing.
Kettie Artigaud for her help with general styling and
furnishing.
Kathleen Jennings for her patience and help throughout the
adaptation and translation of this book.
Monsieur Remande, director of l'Ecole Supérieure de
Cuisine in Paris.
Chef Xavier Vallero and Chef Eric Trochon for permission
to use a selection of their recipes.
Also to Monsieur and Madame Lebain, Monsieur David and
Madame Marie-Solange Bezaunt, Madame Chardot, and
Monsieur Bernard Bouton of Sougé.

CLB 2196
This edition first published in the United States in 1990 by Gallery Books,
an imprint of W.H. Smith Publishers, Inc.,
112 Madison Avenue, New York 10016
© 1990 Colour Library Books Ltd., Godalming, Surrey, England
Typesetting by Acesetters Ltd, Richmond, Surrey, England
Color separations by Coloursplendor Graphics Ltd., Hong Kong
All rights reserved
ISBN 0 8317 1280 5

Gallery Books are available for bulk purchase for sales promotions and
premium use. For details write or telephone the Manager of Special Sales,
W.H. Smith Publishers, Inc.,
112 Madison Avenue, New York, New York 10016. (212) 532-6600

THE TASTE OF
CHINA

Frederic Lebain · Jean Paul Paireault

 Introduction

In the West we talk blithely of "Chinese cooking," as though such a vast country as China might possess one homogenous cuisine. In truth, extreme variations in climate and geography have provided such a wide variety of available ingredients, that many different regional cooking styles have developed. Nevertheless, they have three distinct features in common, and these could be said to characterize a uniform style of Chinese cooking.

The first of the common features is the use of the technique of stir-frying, in which the ingredients are cooked quickly in a small amount of oil at high temperatures. The secret of good stir-frying is preparing all the ingredients carefully beforehand and then cooking them in a particular order, so that in the finished dish each ingredient is cooked and yet retains all its taste, goodness and texture.

The importance of texture in Chinese cooking is the second of its common features. After cooking, vegetables should retain all their crispness, and rice and noodles should still have "bite." The Chinese also use some ingredients which have very little taste in themselves specifically to add different textures to dishes. These include ingredients which are familiar and easily available to Westerners, such as bamboo shoots, water chestnuts and cellophane noodles, and others which are both less readily available and perhaps less immediately appealing to Western palates, such as shark's fin, bird's nest and hair seaweed.

The third common feature is the use of dried foodstuffs. Dried mushrooms, seafood, bean curd, noodles of many varieties, tangerine peel, dates, sausages and, of course, spices are all extremely important in Chinese cooking. Originally developed to preserve foods for out-of-season use, dried products are now used throughout the year in Chinese cooking because they add a fuller flavor to the dish, than the equivalent fresh product.

Beyond these common features, Chinese cooking can be divided into four main styles. Southern or Cantonese cooking, which is perhaps the best known in the West, is characterized by subtle flavors and clear sauces, with rice as the staple accompaniment. Eastern or Shanghai cooking is also lightly seasoned but is much richer, because the meat is marinated beforehand and strongly flavored stocks are used. Western or Szechuan cooking is very highly seasoned and intensely flavored, the area being famous for its peppercorns and chilies. Finally, Northern or Peking cooking uses minimal seasonings, shows Mongolian influences in the popularity of lamb dishes, and favors steamed or roasted breads or noodles as an accompaniment.

Western interest in Chinese cooking is relatively recent and has come about largely through the restaurants initially established by immigrants to service their own communities. Increased travel by Westerners to the East and a growing realization among the health conscious of the benefits of the Chinese style of cooking have increased its popularity. The initial interest has now been followed by a demand from cooks for the means to experiment at home, and authentic Chinese ingredients are becoming more readily available not just in specialty shops but even in supermarkets.

The Taste of China takes all the characteristics of Chinese cooking, both national and regional, and turns them into dishes which are sometimes classic and sometimes inventive interpretations of the classics, inventiveness and individuality being truly representative of the nature of Chinese cooking. The result is a mouthwatering collection of recipes, each presented in an easy-to-follow step-by-step format and accompanied by a color photograph of the finished dish. By not confining itself to one particular style or technique, the broad scope of this book provides the cook with a true taste of China.

―――― SERVES 4 ――――

CRAB SOUP WITH GINGER

This delicately flavored soup, with fresh crab and a hint of ginger,
is perfect for serving at a special dinner.

Step 2

Step 2

Step 2

□ 1 carrot, chopped　　□ 1 onion, chopped　　□ ½ leek, chopped
□ 1 bay leaf　　□ 2 medium-sized crabs　　□ 3 cups fish stock
□ 1-inch piece of fresh ginger root, chopped　　□ 1 tsp sake
□ Salt and pepper

1. Make a vegetable stock by putting the carrot, onion, leek and bay leaf into a saucepan with a large quantity of water. Bring to the boil and add the crabs. Allow to boil briskly for 20 minutes or until cooked.

2. Remove the crabs when cooked and allow to cool. Once cooled, break off the pinchers and break the joints, cut open the back and open the claws. Carefully remove all the crab meat.

3. Bring the fish stock to the boil and add the ginger, sake and the crab meat. Boil for 15 minutes.

4. Check the seasoning, adding salt and pepper as necessary. Serve very hot.

□ TIME　Preparation takes about 40 minutes and cooking takes approximately 35 minutes. It takes about 30 minutes for the crab to cool, before you can comfortably remove the meat with your fingers.

□ CHECKPOINT　Allow plenty of time for opening the crab and removing all the meat. If time does not permit preparing fresh crab, use canned crab meat.

□ COOK'S TIP　Prepare the soup the day before serving. If allowed to rest overnight, the flavors of the soup develop deliciously. Reheat gently just before serving.

□

OPPOSITE

CRAB SOUP
WITH GINGER

CHINESE RAVIOLI

Steamed Chinese ravioli with a stuffing of pork and Chinese cabbage.

Step 2

Step 3

Step 4

□ 1lb pork, finely diced   □ 1 cup Chinese cabbage, finely sliced
□ 1 scallion, chopped   □ 1 tbsp soy sauce   □ Salt and pepper
□ 16 wonton wrappers (Chinese ravioli)   □ 1 egg, beaten
□ 1 tsp sesame oil

1. In a bowl, mix together the pork, Chinese cabbage, scallion and soy sauce. Season with salt and pepper. Leave to marinate for 30 minutes, stirring occasionally.

2. Peel off the wonton wrappers one by one and place a little of the drained stuffing on each. Try not to get any stuffing on the edges of the wrappers.

3. Brush the edges of the wrappers with the beaten egg.

4. Fold them in half, pushing the stuffing into the center and pushing out any trapped air. Seal the edges well with your fingers and then cut off any excess dough with a knife or a pastry cutter.

5. Cook the ravioli on a damp kitchen towel in a Chinese steamer for approximately 15 minutes. Turn over once during cooking and brush with the sesame oil.

6. If you have any stuffing left over, stir-fry it quickly in a little hot oil and serve with the ravioli.

□ TIME   Preparation takes about 20 minutes and cooking takes approximately 25 minutes.

□ CHECKPOINT   It is very important to seal the edges of the ravioli firmly before steaming, otherwise the stuffing will leak out.

□ COOK'S TIP   Any excess dough trimmed off in Step 4, can be cut into small pieces and added to a soup.

□

OPPOSITE

CHINESE RAVIOLI

——— SERVES 4 ———

ABALONE SOUP

Canned abalone cooked in fish stock and flavored with oyster and
soy sauces – absolutely delicious.

Step 2

Step 2

☐ 3 cups fish stock ☐ 6 canned abalone + 2 tbsps reserved juice
☐ ½ scallion, chopped ☐ 1 tbsp soy sauce ☐ ½ tbsp oyster sauce
☐ 1 egg white ☐ Salt and pepper

1. Heat together the fish stock, the reserved abalone juice, scallion, soy sauce and the oyster sauce.

2. Cut the canned abalone first into thin slices and then into matchsticks. Add to the stock and simmer gently for 15 minutes.

3. Beat the egg white lightly and then stir it gradually into the boiling soup.

4. Season with salt and pepper to taste and serve.

☐ TIME   Preparation takes about 5 minutes and cooking time is approximately 15 minutes.

☐ VARIATION   The fish stock can be replaced with chicken stock.

☐ WATCHPOINT   The egg white should be lightly beaten and added to the boiling soup slowly, so that it thickens immediately.

☐

OPPOSITE

ABALONE SOUP

─── SERVES 4 ───

SPRING ROLLS

*Stuffed spring rolls, served slightly chilled,
make a wonderful appetizer.*

Step 7

Step 7

Step 7

☐ 1 large pork chop, cooked   ☐ 8oz cooked chicken   ☐ 1 tsp soy sauce   ☐ 1 tsp sugar   ☐ 2 tbsps sesame oil   ☐ ¼ cup bamboo shoots, blanched   ☐ 1 cup bean sprouts   ☐ 1 Chinese mushroom, soaked for 15 minutes in warm water and sliced thinly   ☐ 1 tsp cornstarch, combined with a little water   ☐ 18 square sheets rice paper, soaked in water

FOR THE SAUCE

☐ 2 tbsps water   ☐ Juice of ½ lemon   ☐ 1 tsp sugar   ☐ 1 clove garlic, chopped 2 tbsps each carrot and zucchini, cut into thin strips   ☐ 2 tbsps fish sauce

1. Remove the pork from the bone and cut into thin strips.

2. Cut the cooked chicken into thin strips.

3. Mix the two meats together with the soy sauce, sugar and 1 tbsp of the sesame oil. Allow to marinate until required.

4. Heat the remaining sesame oil in a wok and stir-fry the bamboo shoots, bean sprouts and mushroom. Cook until tender.

5. Add the meat mixture and the marinade to the wok. Stir well and heat through.

6. Thicken the contents of the wok by stirring in the cornstarch. Set the wok aside and allow the contents to cool completely.

7. Drain the rice paper sheets. Place a little stuffing on each of the sheets. Fold up the bottom half of each sheet, then fold over the side flaps. Finally, roll up each sheet, beginning at the bottom where the stuffing is visible, and seal the edges by brushing lightly with water. Allow the rolls to dry. Chill in the refrigerator.

8. Mix together the sauce ingredients and serve with the rolls.

☐ TIME   Preparation takes about 25 minutes and cooking takes approximately 15 minutes.

☐ COOK'S TIP   If time permits, it is better to stir-fry the bean sprouts, mushrooms and bamboo shoots separately and then mix them all together just before placing the stuffing on the rice paper.

☐ SERVING IDEA   Serve with shredded lettuce leaves.

☐

OPPOSITE

SPRING ROLLS

─── SERVES 4 ───

CHICKEN AND CORN SOUP

*This soup uses baby corn on the cob and chicken and is flavored
with ginger and soy sauce.*

Step 2

Step 3

Step 4

□ ¾ cup canned corn   □ 3 cups chicken stock   □ 2 chicken breasts,
cooked   □ 12 baby corn on the cob   □ 1-inch piece of fresh ginger
root, chopped   □ 2 tbsps light soy sauce   □ Pinch monosodium
glutamate   □ Few drops chili sauce   □ Salt and pepper

1. Place the canned corn in a food processor with ½ cup of the chicken
stock. Process until smooth.

2. Strain the purée through a sieve, pushing it through with the help of
a spoon.

3. Cut the chicken into thin slices and stir them into the remaining
stock, in a saucepan.

4. Stir in the corn purée.

5. Add the baby corn and bring to the boil. Simmer for 15 minutes. Add
the ginger, soy sauce, and monosodium glutamate. Continue cooking
for another 10 minutes.

6. Add a few drops of chili sauce. Check the seasoning, adding salt and
pepper if necessary and serve.

□ TIME   Preparation takes about 5 minutes and cooking takes
approximately 25 minutes.

□ COOK'S TIP   Prepare the soup the day before serving to give the
flavors time to develop.

□ VARIATION   Creamed corn can be used instead of the processed
corn.

□

OPPOSITE

CHICKEN AND
CORN SOUP

—— SERVES 4 ——

RICE SOUP

A tasty, economical soup which uses leftover meat.

Step 3

Step 4

☐ 4 dried Chinese mushrooms, soaked in warm water for 15 minutes   ☐ 3 cups duck stock   ☐ 1 scallion, chopped   ☐ 2 tbsps canned corn   ☐ ½ cup leftover meat, chopped into small cubes   ☐ Pinch ground ginger   ☐ 1 tbsp sake   ☐ 1 tbsp soy sauce   ☐ Salt and pepper   ☐ ½ cup cooked rice

1. Drain the mushrooms and slice thinly, discarding the stalks.

2. Place the mushrooms in a saucepan with the duck stock and the scallion.

3. Add the corn, meat, ginger, sake, soy sauce, and salt and pepper to taste. Bring to the boil and simmer briskly for 10 minutes.

4. Stir in the rice and cook for 1 minute. Check the seasoning, adjusting as necessary, and serve.

☐ TIME   Preparation takes about 5 minutes and cooking takes approximately 12 minutes.

☐ VARIATION   You can use any sort of meat in this soup: beef, chicken, pork, etc.

☐ CHECKPOINT   If you do not like your rice too soft, add half-cooked rice, which will then finish cooking in the soup.

☐

OPPOSITE

RICE SOUP

---- SERVES 4 ----

TURKEY SOUP WITH BLACK MUSHROOMS

An unusual blend of flavors which makes a tasty, warming soup.

☐ 6oz turkey breast ☐ 1 tbsp sesame oil ☐ 2oz dried Chinese black mushrooms, soaked for 15 minutes in warm water
☐ 3 cups chicken stock ☐ 1 tbsp soy sauce ☐ 1 slice fresh root ginger ☐ Salt and pepper

Step 1

Step 1

1. Cut the turkey meat into slices and then into small cubes.

2. Heat the sesame oil in a wok and stir-fry the meat until brown. Remove from the pan and drain off any excess oil.

3. Cook the mushrooms in boiling, salted water for 10 minutes. Rinse and drain well.

4. Place the mushrooms in a saucepan with the stock. Stir in the meat, soy sauce, ginger and salt and pepper to taste.

5. Bring to the boil and then simmer gently for 15 minutes.

6. Serve the soup piping hot.

☐ TIME   Preparation takes about 8 minutes and cooking takes approximately 35 minutes.

☐ SERVING IDEA   Sprinkle the soup with 1 tbsp chopped fresh chives before serving.

☐ CHECKPOINT   Don't forget to remove the slice of ginger before serving.

☐

OPPOSITE

TURKEY SOUP
WITH BLACK
MUSHROOMS

───── SERVES 4 ─────

BEEF AND NOODLE SOUP

*Marinated beef is sliced and cooked in beef stock with noodles
to make a rich and extremely filling soup.*

Step 1

Step 1

☐ 8oz fillet of beef   ☐ ½ tsp chopped garlic   ☐ 1 scallion, chopped
☐ 2 tbsps soy sauce   ☐ Salt and pepper   ☐ 8oz fresh noodles
☐ Few drops sesame oil   ☐ 3 cups beef stock   ☐ Few drops chili sauce
☐ 1 tbsp chopped chives

1. Cut the beef into thin slices. Sprinkle the chopped garlic and scallion over the meat. Finally, sprinkle over the soy sauce and season with salt and pepper. Marinate the meat for 15 minutes.

2. Cook the noodles in boiling, salted water to which a few drops of sesame oil have been added. Rinse them in cold water and set aside to drain.

3. Bring the beef stock to the boil and add the beef and the marinade. Simmer gently for 10 minutes.

4. Stir in the noodles, season with a few drops of chili sauce and simmer just long enough to heat the noodles through.

5. Serve with the chives sprinkled over the top.

☐   TIME   Preparation takes about 5 minutes, marinating time is 15 minutes and cooking takes approximately 12 minutes.

☐   VARIATION   If you used a marrowbone to make the stock, add a little chopped beef marrow to the soup, just before serving.

☐   WATCHPOINT   Do not overcook the noodles; they should still be quite firm at the end of Step 2.

☐

OPPOSITE

BEEF AND
NOODLE SOUP

—— SERVES 4 ——

CHICKEN AND BEAN SPROUT SOUP

A quickly prepared, aromatic soup with chicken and bean sprouts.

Step 2

Step 3

☐ 1 cup cooked boneless chicken ☐ 3 cups bean sprouts ☐ 3 cups chicken stock ☐ 1 tbsp white wine vinegar ☐ 2 tsps sugar ☐ 2 tbsps soy sauce ☐ 1 tbsp chopped onion ☐ 2 shallots, chopped ☐ Salt and pepper

1. Cut the chicken meat into small cubes.

2. Put the bean sprouts and the stock into a saucepan and bring to the boil.

3. Reduce the heat and add the meat, vinegar, sugar, soy sauce, onion, shallots and salt and pepper to taste.

4. Stir well and cook the soup for 15 minutes over a moderate heat. Serve hot.

☐ TIME   Preparation takes about 4 minutes and cooking takes approximately 15 minutes.

☐ VARIATION   The chopped onion could be replaced with scallion.

☐ CHECKPOINT   The bean sprouts should still be slightly crunchy when the soup is cooked.

☐

OPPOSITE

CHICKEN AND
BEAN SPROUT
SOUP

─── SERVES 4 ───

FISH AND RICE SOUP

This fish soup is delicately flavored with ginger and contains
finely sliced fish and rice.

Step 2

Step 2

☐ 3 cups fish stock   ☐ 1 tbsp soy sauce   ☐ 1 slice fresh ginger root, chopped   ☐ 12oz fresh cod or haddock fillet   ☐ ½ tsp cornstarch, combined with a little water   ☐ ½ cup rice, part-cooked
☐ Salt and pepper

1. Heat together the fish stock, soy sauce and ginger.

2. Cut the fish fillet first into very thin slices and then into strips.

3. Stir the cornstarch into the stock and simmer gently for 10 minutes.

4. Stir in the drained, precooked rice and cook for 5 minutes.

5. Remove from the heat and add the fish.

6. Allow the fish to cook for several minutes in the hot soup. Check the seasoning, adding salt and pepper as necessary and serve immediately.

☐ TIME   Preparation takes about 5 minutes and cooking takes approximately 15 minutes.

☐ VARIATION   Any variety of fish could be used in this recipe, but remember to slice it very thinly.

☐ COOK'S TIP   The rice should have been part cooked in boiling, lightly salted water for approximately 3 minutes, before being used in this recipe.

☐

OPPOSITE

FISH AND RICE
SOUP

——— SERVES 4 ———

CHINESE OMELET

A chicken, ham and shrimp omelet, flavored with chopped chives.

Step 1

Step 2

☐ 8 eggs, beaten   ☐ 2 slices ham, chopped   ☐ 1 cup cooked chicken meat   ☐ 8 cooked shrimp, peeled and chopped
☐ 1 tbsp chopped chives   ☐ ½ tbsp soy sauce   ☐ 2 tbsps oil
☐ Salt and pepper

1. Mix together the eggs, ham, chicken and shrimp.

2. Stir in the chives and soy sauce. Check the seasoning, adding salt and pepper to taste.

3. Heat the oil in a frying pan. Add the omelet mixture.

4. Gently stir the omelet with a fork as it is cooking in the frying pan.

5. Fold over first one side of the omelet and then the other, using the tines of the fork to shape it. Serve hot.

☐ TIME   Preparation takes 8 minutes and cooking takes approximately 6-10 minutes.

☐ VARIATION   This omelet can be made with a variety of herbs and cooked meats.

☐

OPPOSITE

CHINESE OMELET

—— SERVES 4 ——

FISH SOUP WITH SURPRISE WONTONS

*Chinese ravioli stuffed with shrimp and cooked
in a fish-flavored soup.*

Step 4

Step 4

Step 4

□ 3 cups fish stock   □ 12 fresh shrimp, peeled and heads removed,
peelings and heads set aside   □ 1 tbsp oil   □ ½ tsp chopped parsley
□ Pinch chopped garlic   □ Salt and pepper   □ 12 wonton wrappers
□ 1 egg, beaten   □ 1 tbsp soy sauce

1. In a saucepan, bring the fish stock to the boil together with the
reserved heads and peelings from the shrimp. Boil gently for
15 minutes. Strain through a fine sieve, reserving only the stock.

2. Heat the oil in a wok and stir-fry four of the shrimp, cut into small
pieces, together with the parsley, garlic and salt and pepper to taste.
Allow to cool.

3. Spread out the wonton wrappers and place a little of the above
stuffing on each one.

4. Brush the beaten egg all around the edges of the dough. Fold one
side over onto the other, cut the ravioli into the desired shape and seal
well by pinching the edges together firmly. Set the ravioli aside to rest
for 10 minutes.

5. Bring the stock back to the boil, then add the remaining shrimp and
the soy sauce. Pinch once more round the edges of the ravioli, then slip
them into the stock. Season with salt and pepper and simmer briskly
for 5 minutes.

6. Serve piping hot.

□ TIME   Preparation takes about 20 minutes, resting time for the
ravioli is 10 minutes and cooking takes approximately 20 minutes.

□ VARIATION   You could replace the shrimp in this recipe with any
type of shellfish.

□ WATCHPOINT   Pinch together the edges of the ravioli very firmly,
so that none of the stuffing escapes during cooking. Do not, however,
brush on too much egg, or the dough will soften.

□

OPPOSITE

FISH SOUP
WITH SURPRISE
WONTONS

CLEAR CHICKEN SOUP
WITH EGG

*A tasty soup based on chicken stock with lots of flavor-enhancing
ingredients and served with a poached egg.*

Step 2

Step 3

Step 4

□ 4 dried Chinese mushrooms, soaked 15 minutes in warm water
□ 1 tbsp coarse sea salt   □ 1 tbsp wine vinegar   □ 1 bay leaf
□ 4 eggs   □ 3 cups chicken stock   □ 1 onion, chopped
□ 10 chives   □ 1 tbsp soy sauce   □ Few drops chili sauce
□ Salt and pepper

1. Cook the mushrooms in boiling, salted water for 15 minutes, rinse in fresh water and set aside to drain. Cut them into thin slices.

2. Set a large saucepan of water to boil, with the sea salt, vinegar and bay leaf.

3. When the water is boiling, reduce to a gentle simmer and carefully break in the eggs one at a time.

4. Poach the eggs for 1 minute and then remove them from the boiling water with a slotted spoon. Drain on a tea towel.

5. Heat the stock in a saucepan with the onion, bring to the boil and simmer for 10 minutes.

6. Strain the stock through a fine sieve, discarding the onion. Check the seasoning, adding salt and pepper as necessary.

7. Bring the stock back to the boil and add the mushrooms, chives, soy sauce and a few drops of chili sauce. Cook for 10 minutes. One minute before serving add the eggs.

□ TIME   Preparation takes about 10 minutes, reconstituting the mushrooms 15 minutes and cooking takes approximately 10 minutes.

□ VARIATION   Replace the chicken eggs with quail eggs.

□ COOK'S TIP   The vinegar is not used in this recipe to add flavor, but to prevent the eggs turning brown.

□

OPPOSITE

CLEAR CHICKEN
SOUP WITH EGG

───── SERVES 4 ─────

BAMBOO SHOOT SOUP

A very decorative soup. Beaten egg sifted into the hot soup gives a very special effect.

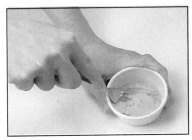

Step 5

Step 5

Step 5

☐ ½ cup bamboo shoots, cut into thin matchsticks   ☐ 4 dried Chinese black mushrooms, soaked for 15 minutes in warm water   ☐ 3 cups chicken stock   ☐ 1 tbsp wine vinegar   ☐ 2 tbsps light soy sauce   ☐ Salt and pepper   ☐ ½ tsp cornstarch, combined with a little water   ☐ 1 egg   ☐ 10 chives

1. Blanch the bamboo shoots in boiling, salted water for 3 minutes. Rinse and set aside to drain.

2. Cook the mushrooms in boiling, salted water for 10 minutes. Rinse and set aside to drain.

3. Bring the stock to the boil and add the bamboo shoots, mushrooms, vinegar, and soy sauce and season with salt and pepper to taste. Cook for 10 minutes.

4. Stir in the cornstarch and bring the soup slowly back to the boil.

5. Reduce the heat. Beat the egg thoroughly. Place the beaten egg in a sieve and add to the soup by shaking the sieve back and forth over the hot soup.

6. Add the chives to the soup and serve piping hot.

☐ TIME   Preparation takes about 5 minutes and cooking takes approximately 30 minutes.

☐ CHECKPOINT   Make sure the soup is boiling hot before adding the beaten egg.

☐ COOK'S TIP   Try to buy fresh chives for this soup, as they have a much better flavor than dried chives.

☐

<u>OPPOSITE</u>

BAMBOO SHOOT
SOUP

—— SERVES 4 ——

LAMB AND NOODLE SOUP

*A hearty soup based on a good stock with mushrooms
and tender lamb.*

Step 1

□ 4oz transparent noodles   □ 6 dried Chinese mushrooms, soaked
for 15 minutes in warm water   □ 3 cups lamb stock, skimmed
□ 6oz lamb, sliced   □ 1 tbsp soy sauce   □ Few drops chili sauce
□ Salt and pepper

1. Break the transparent noodles into small pieces and cook them in boiling, salted water for 20 seconds. Rinse them in fresh water and set aside to drain.

2. Cook the mushrooms in boiling, lightly salted water for 15 minutes, rinse them in fresh water and set aside to drain.

3. Cut the mushrooms into thin slices.

4. Heat the lamb stock in a saucepan and add the lamb, mushrooms, soy sauce and a few drops of chili sauce.

5. Season with salt and pepper and simmer gently for 15 minutes.

6. Stir in the drained noodles and simmer just long enough for the noodles to heat through. Serve immediately.

□ TIME   Preparation takes about 5 minutes, reconstituting the mushrooms about 15 minutes and cooking takes approximately 30 minutes.

□ VARIATION   Use fresh Chinese noodles instead of the transparent noodles.

□ COOK'S TIP   If the noodles are too hard to break with your fingers, use a serrated knife to cut them.

□

OPPOSITE

LAMB AND
NOODLE SOUP

─────── SERVES 4 ───────

SHRIMP OMELETS

These light and tasty omelets are flavored with garlic, shallot, chives and shrimp.

Step 4

Step 4

☐ 8 shrimp, peeled   ☐ 1 tbsp oil   ☐ ½ tsp chopped garlic
☐ ½ tsp chopped shallot   ☐ 8 eggs, beaten   ☐ 4 tbsps chopped chives
☐ 4 tbsps oil   ☐ Salt and pepper

1. Cut the peeled shrimp into small pieces.

2. Heat the 1 tbsp oil in a small frying pan and fry the shrimp with the garlic and shallot until golden brown. Set aside.

3. Beat together the eggs and the chives. In a frying pan, cook several thin omelets, using a little of the 4 tbsps oil for each one.

4. Cut rounds out of the cooked omelets using a pastry cutter or a glass. Layer these rounds with the shrimp filling.

5. Serve hot, either whole or cut into wedges.

☐ TIME   Preparation takes about 10 minutes and cooking takes approximately 20 minutes.

☐ SERVING IDEA   You could serve this dish cold with a tossed mixed salad.

☐ COOK'S TIP   The omelets should be quite thin, like crepes.

☐

OPPOSITE

SHRIMP OMELETS

---- SERVES 4 ----

PEKING STYLE SOUP

*Duck stock is the basis of this tasty, filling soup, which
contains meat and vegetables, the whole delicately flavored
with sesame seeds and soy sauce.*

Step 1

Step 1

□ 4 slices smoked ham   □ 4 cups Chinese cabbage   □ 3 cups
duck stock   □ 1 tbsp sesame seeds   □ Pinch chopped garlic
□ 1 tbsp soy sauce   □ ½ tsp white wine vinegar   □ Salt and pepper
□ 1 egg yolk, beaten

1. Cut the ham into small, even-sized cubes.

2. Cut the Chinese cabbage into small pieces and simmer briskly for 10 minutes in the duck stock.

3. Stir in the sesame seeds, garlic, ham, soy sauce, vinegar and salt and pepper to taste.

4. Cook for 10 minutes over a gentle heat. Using a teaspoon, drizzle the beaten egg yolk into the soup. Serve immediately.

□   TIME   Preparation takes about 5 minutes and cooking takes approximately 20 minutes.

□   VARIATION   Replace the smoked ham with a different smoked meat.

□   CHECKPOINT   The smoked ham is likely to change color during cooking.

□

OPPOSITE

PEKING STYLE
SOUP

SERVES 4

FISH SOUP WITH CORN

*Home-made fish stock is the basis of a soup to which corn and
sliced, filleted fish are added.*

Step 1

Step 1

Step 1

☐ 1 tbsp oil   ☐ 1 carrot, chopped   ☐ 1 onion, chopped   ☐ ½ leek,
chopped   ☐ 1 bay leaf   ☐ 2¼lbs mixed fish   ☐ 2 trout fillets
☐ 1 cod or fresh haddock fillet   ☐ 2 tbsps oyster sauce   ☐ 1 tbsp soy
sauce   ☐ ½ tsp cornstarch, combined with a little water
☐ 1 cup canned corn   ☐ Salt and pepper

1. To make the fish stock, heat the oil in a large saucepan and gently fry
the carrot, onion, leek and bay leaf. When the vegetables are nicely
colored, add the 2¼lbs mixed fish, together with all the heads and
bones. Cover with water and boil for 30 minutes.

2. Strain through a fine sieve, reserving only the stock and discarding
all the rest.

3. Slice the trout and cod or haddock fillets thinly crosswise and set
them aside.

4. Measure 3 cups of fish stock into a saucepan and bring it to the boil.

5. Stir in the oyster sauce, soy sauce, cornstarch and the corn.

6. Boil for 10 minutes, then turn off the heat and add the sliced fish.

7. Check the seasoning, adding salt and pepper as necessary. Allow to
stand for 1 minute before serving.

☐ TIME   Preparation takes about 5 minutes, cooking, including
cooking the stock, takes approximately 40 minutes.

☐ COOK'S TIP   To make the fish stock, use a mixture of the most
economical varieties of fish, discarding nothing.

☐ WATCHPOINT   If the soup is still at boiling point when the fish is
added at Step 6, it will be hot enough to cook the fish, providing this
has been cut into thin slices.

☐

OPPOSITE

FISH SOUP
WITH CORN

───── SERVES 4 ─────

IMPERIAL PORK ROLLS

These fried rice paper rolls are stuffed with a mixture of bean sprouts, black mushrooms and pork and served with a spicy fish sauce.

Step 4

Step 5

□ ½ tbsp vinegar   □ 1 tbsp water   □ 1 tbsp fish sauce   □ 1 tsp sugar
□ ½ tsp chopped fresh ginger root   □ Chili sauce   □ 4 dried
Chinese black mushrooms, soaked for 15 minutes in warm water
□ 12oz boned pork shoulder, very finely chopped   □ ½ tsp oil
□ ½ cup bean sprouts, blanched and drained   □ ½ tsp cornstarch
□ 1 tbsp soy sauce   □ Salt and pepper   □ 16 sheets rice paper,
soaked in warm water for 10 minutes   □ A little beaten egg
□ ½ cup oil

1. To make the sauce, mix together the vinegar, water, fish sauce, sugar and ginger and allow to stand for 30 minutes. Add a few drops of chili sauce, just before serving.

2. Dice the mushrooms very finely and mix them with the meat.

3. Heat the ½ tsp oil in a wok and stir-fry the above together with the bean sprouts, soy sauce and cornstarch for 2 minutes. Allow to cool. The mixture should be quite dry. Add salt, pepper and chili sauce to taste.

4. Drain the rice paper sheets and spread them out on your work surface. Place a little of the cooled stuffing in the center of each sheet, roll it up and seal the edges with a little of the beaten egg.

5. Heat the ½ cup oil in a wok and fry the rolls gently on all sides, beginning with the sealed side. Drain on paper towels.

6. Serve the rolls hot, with the sauce in individual bowls.

□ TIME   Preparation takes about 30 minutes and cooking takes approximately 15 minutes.

□ SERVING IDEA   Serve the rolls with lettuce leaves and fresh mint. Guests should wrap the mint and lettuce leaves around the rolls, before dipping them into the sauce.

□

OPPOSITE

IMPERIAL PORK
ROLLS

—— SERVES 4 ——

NOODLES WITH GINGER AND OYSTER SAUCE

Noodles stir-fried with ginger, carrot and zucchini, then served in an oyster sauce.

Step 3

Step 3

Step 3

☐ 8oz Chinese noodles   ☐ 1 carrot   ☐ 1 zucchini   ☐ 3 slices fresh ginger root   ☐ 1 scallion, cut into thin rounds   ☐ 1 tbsp oil ☐ 1 tbsp soy sauce   ☐ 2 tbsps oyster sauce   ☐ Salt and pepper

1. Cook the noodles in boiling, salted water, rinse them under cold water, and set aside to drain.

2. Cut the carrot into thin strips. Thickly peel the zucchini to include a little of the flesh and cut into thin strips. Discard the center of the zucchini.

3. Peel the fresh ginger root sparingly, but remove any hard parts. Slice thinly, using a potato peeler. Cut the slices into thin strips, using a very sharp knife. Heat the oil in a wok, and stir-fry the scallion for 10 seconds; add the carrot, zucchini and ginger, and stir-fry briefly.

4. Stir in the noodles and cook for 1 minute.

5. Stir in the soy and oyster sauces, and continue cooking until heated through. Season with salt and pepper and serve.

☐ TIME   Preparation takes about 15 minutes and cooking takes approximately 15 minutes.

☐ VARIATION   Cook the noodles in chicken stock instead of salted water to give them extra flavor.

☐ CHECKPOINT   Stir-fry the ginger and the other vegetables very quickly, to avoid browning them. Lower the heat if necessary.

☐

OPPOSITE

NOODLES WITH GINGER AND OYSTER SAUCE

———— SERVES 4 ————

RICE PAPER PARCELS WITH ABALONE

Step 4

Step 5

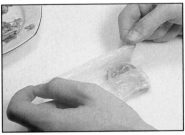
Step 5

Step 6

□ 12 sheets of rice paper, brushed with or dipped in warm water and then drained   □ 8oz canned abalone   □ 4 tbsps oil   □ ½ tsp each chopped fresh ginger root and garlic · □ ½ scallion, finely diced   □ ¼ cucumber   □ ½ green pepper, seeded and finely diced   □ 1 cup fresh bean sprouts   □ 1 tbsp soy sauce   □ Salt and pepper

FOR THE SAUCE

□ 1 tbsp soy sauce   □ 2 tsps wine vinegar   □ ½ tsp sugar   □ Salt and pepper

1. Cut 12 thin slices from the abalone. Cut the remaining abalone into small dice.

2. Heat 1 tbsp of the oil in a wok and stir-fry the garlic, ginger, diced abalone, scallion, cucumber, pepper, bean sprouts and soy sauce for 5 minutes.

3. Remove from the wok and set aside to cool.

4. Spread out the rice paper sheets and divide the above stuffing evenly between them, placing it in the center of each sheet.

5. Fold up first one side and then the other over the stuffing.

6. Next, fold in both ends to form 12 square parcels.

7. Heat 2 tbsps of the oil in a frying pan and gently cook the sliced abalone for a few minutes on both sides.

8. Heat the remaining oil and fry the rice paper parcels on both sides until golden brown. Drain on paper towels.

9. Mix together the sauce ingredients and serve the sauce in little individual bowls, to accompany the fried parcels and the sliced abalone.

□ TIME   Preparation takes about 25 minutes and cooking takes approximately 10 minutes.

SERVING IDEA The parcels could be made larger or smaller, as desired.

□ COOK'S TIP   Use square sheets of rice paper for this recipe, as they are much easier to fold up neatly than the round sheets.

□

OPPOSITE

RICE PAPER PARCELS WITH ABALONE

STIR-FRIED RICE WITH PEPPERS

Long grain rice stir-fried with red and green peppers, onions and soy sauce.

Step 2

Step 3

□ ¾ cup long grain rice   □ 1 tbsp peanut oil   □ 1 onion, chopped
□ 1 green pepper, seeded and cut into small pieces   □ 1 red pepper,
seeded and cut into small pieces   □ 1 tbsp soy sauce   □ Salt and
pepper   □ 1 tsp sesame oil

1. Cook the rice in boiling water, drain and set aside.

2. Heat the oil in a wok and stir-fry the onion, add the peppers and fry until lightly browned.

3. Add the rice to the wok, stir in the soy sauce and continue cooking until the rice is heated through completely.

4. Season with salt, pepper and the sesame oil and serve.

□ TIME   Preparation takes 5 minutes and cooking takes approximately 25 minutes.

□ VARIATION   If you like the strong flavor of sesame oil, stir-fry the vegetables and rice in this instead of the peanut oil.

□ CHECKPOINT   Do not overcook the rice in Step 1, or it will become sticky in Step 3.

□

OPPOSITE

STIR-FRIED RICE
WITH PEPPERS

———— SERVES 4 ————

CELLOPHANE NOODLES WITH SHRIMP

An oyster and wine sauce enhances this light and tasty seafood dish.

Step 2

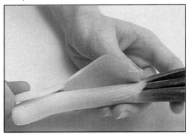

Step 2

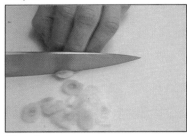

Step 2

☐ 9oz cellophane noodles   ☐ 1 scallion   ☐ 1 tbsp oil   ☐ 24 fresh shrimp, peeled   ☐ 1 tbsp Chinese wine   ☐ 2 tbsps light soy sauce   ☐ ½ tsp sugar   ☐ 1 tbsp oyster sauce.   ☐ ¼ cup fish stock   ☐ Few drops sesame oil

1. Cook the noodles in boiling, salted water for 1 minute. Drain and rinse under cold water. Set aside to drain.

2. To prepare the scallion, slice off the roots and peel off the tough outer leaves before slicing the scallion into thin rounds. Heat the oil in a wok and stir-fry the scallion and the shrimp for 1 minute.

3. Reduce the heat, drain off the excess fat, and deglaze the wok with the Chinese wine.

4. Stir in the drained noodles, soy sauce, sugar, oyster sauce, fish stock and sesame oil.

5. Cook until the noodles are heated through and then serve immediately.

☐ TIME   Preparation takes about 15 minutes and cooking takes approximately 15 minutes.

☐ VARIATION   The fresh shrimp could be replaced with cooked ones.

☐ CHECKPOINT   When adding the noodles to the wok, the heat must be reduced considerably, or the noodles will be overcooked.

☐

OPPOSITE

CELLOPHANE
NOODLES WITH
SHRIMP

FRIED NOODLES WITH PORK AND VEGETABLES

Fried noodles, served with pork and vegetables in a rich, tasty sauce.

Step 1

Step 1

Step 1

☐ 12oz fresh noodles   ☐ 1 taro   ☐ 1 tbsp oil   ☐ 1 tsp chopped garlic   ☐ 1 carrot, cut into sticks   ☐ 1 cup Chinese cabbage, sliced thinly   ☐ 1 cup thinly sliced, cooked pork   ☐ 1 tbsp soy sauce   ☐ 1¼ cups chicken stock   ☐ Salt and pepper   ☐ Oil for deep-frying   ☐ 1 tsp cornstarch, combined with a little water

1. Cook the noodles in boiling, salted water, rinse in warm water and set aside to drain. Prepare the taro by first slicing off the end then peeling with a potato peeler. Lastly, using the potato peeler, cut the taro into thin slices.

2. Heat the oil in a wok and stir-fry the taro, garlic, carrot and Chinese cabbage.

3. Add the pork, soy sauce, stock, and salt and pepper. Cook over a gentle heat for 5 minutes, shaking the wok frequently.

4. Heat the oil for deep-frying to 350°F and fry the noodles a few at a time. Drain the noodles on paper towels.

5. Share the noodles equally between four small plates.

6. Strain the vegetable and pork mixture from the wok and serve over the noodles.

7. Stir the cornstarch into the remaining sauce in the wok, stirring until the sauce thickens. Pour some over each plate of noodles and serve immediately.

☐ TIME   Preparation takes about 15 minutes and cooking takes approximately 25 minutes.

☐ COOK'S TIP   As the noodles are fried, place them in an ovenproof dish in a warm oven, so that they will stay crisp while cooking the rest of the dish.

☐ CHECKPOINT   Make sure the noodles are completely dry before cooking them in the oil, to avoid spattering.

☐

OPPOSITE

FRIED NOODLES WITH PORK AND VEGETABLES

---------- SERVES 4 ----------

NOODLES WITH PEPPERS
AND GINGER

Chinese noodles with stir-fried peppers, ginger and garlic.

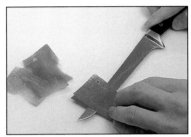

Step 2

Step 3

□ 1 red pepper, seeded   □ 1 green pepper, seeded   □ 8oz Chinese noodles   □ 1 tbsp oil   □ 1 tsp each chopped fresh ginger root and garlic   □ Salt and pepper

1. Cut the peppers into six pieces.

2. Cut each of these pieces in half, to form slices.

3. Cut each slice into very thin matchsticks.

4. Cook the noodles in boiling, lightly salted water, stirring occasionally so that they do not stick.

5. Drain the noodles in a sieve and pass under cold running water. Set aside to drain.

6. Heat the oil in a wok and stir-fry the peppers, ginger and garlic for 1 minute, stirring continuously.

7. Add the well-drained noodles and stir-fry until the noodles are hot. Season to taste and serve immediately.

□ TIME   Preparation takes about 15 minutes, and cooking takes approximately 10 minutes.

□ VARIATION   If you have no fresh ginger root, substitute powdered ginger.

□ CHECKPOINT   If the noodles stick together, run them under hot water until they separate, then drain off the water and continue with Step 7.

□

OPPOSITE

NOODLES WITH PEPPERS AND GINGER

STIR-FRIED STICKY RICE

*Glutinous rice cooked with stir-fried mushrooms,
ginger and scallions.*

Step 4

Step 4

☐ 1¼ cups glutinous rice ☐ 2 tbsps oil ☐ 2 scallions, chopped
☐ ½ onion, chopped ☐ 1 slice fresh ginger root ☐ 4 dried Chinese
black mushrooms, soaked for 15 minutes in warm water, drained
and sliced ☐ Salt and pepper

1. Wash the rice in plenty of cold water and place it in a sieve. Pour 5½ cups boiling water over the rice.

2. Heat the oil in a wok and fry the scallions, onion and ginger until golden brown.

3. Add the mushrooms and continue cooking, stirring and shaking the wok frequently.

4. Add the rice and stir well. Pour over enough water to cover the rice by ½ inch.

5. Cover and cook over a moderate heat until there is almost no liquid left. Reduce the heat once again and continue cooking until all the liquid has been absorbed. This takes approximately 20 minutes in total.

6. Add salt and pepper to taste and serve immediately.

☐ TIME Preparation takes 5 minutes and cooking takes approximately 25 minutes.

☐ VARIATION Replace the water with beef stock to give the rice more flavor.

☐ CHECKPOINT Remove the ginger before serving the rice, as it is only used to flavor the dish.

☐

OPPOSITE

STIR-FRIED
STICKY RICE

─── SERVES 4 ───

CHOW MEIN

*Chinese noodles with bacon and mushrooms, served in a soy
and chicken flavored sauce.*

Step 3

Step 3

□ 6 dried black Chinese mushrooms, soaked for 15 minutes in warm
water   □ 8oz Chinese noodles   □ ¾ cup bacon   □ 1 tbsp oil
□ 1 onion, finely chopped   □ 1 tbsp soy sauce   □ ¼ cup chicken
stock   □ Salt and pepper

1. Drain the mushrooms and slice them thinly.

2. Cook the noodles in boiling, salted water, rinse under cold water
and set aside to drain.

3. Cut the bacon into strips. Then cut the strips into small rectangular
pieces. Heat the oil in a wok and stir-fry the mushrooms, onion and
bacon for 1 minute.

4. Stir in the noodles, soy sauce, chicken stock, salt and pepper. Allow
to heat through completely and serve.

□ TIME   Preparation takes about 5 minutes and cooking takes
approximately 15 minutes.

□ VARIATION   There are many different shapes of Chinese noodles
and any of these can be used in this recipe.

□

OPPOSITE

CHOW MEIN

FRIED NOODLES WITH SHRIMP

Deep-fried noodles served with a richly flavored shrimp sauce.

Step 6

☐ 8oz fresh noodles   ☐ 2 tbsps oil   ☐ 1 red pepper, seeded and cut into small pieces   ☐ 1 tsp chopped garlic   ☐ 20 shrimp, peeled and tails left on   ☐ 1 drop vinegar   ☐ ¼ cup orange juice   ☐ ¼ tsp five-spice powder   ☐ 1 cup fish stock   ☐ 1 tsp cornstarch, combined with a little water   ☐ Salt and pepper   ☐ Oil for deep-frying

1. Cook the noodles in boiling, salted water, then rinse in warm water, and set aside to drain.

2. Heat the oil in a wok and stir-fry the pepper and garlic.

3. Add the shrimp and cook until crisp.

4. Stir in the vinegar, orange juice, five-spice powder and stock, and cook for 5 minutes.

5. Thicken the sauce by adding the cornstarch and stirring continuously. Season with salt and pepper.

6. Heat the oil for deep-frying to 350° F, plunge in the noodles and fry them for 2 minutes, then drain them on paper towels.

7. Serve the noodles hot with the shrimp sauce.

☐ TIME   Preparation takes about 20 minutes and cooking takes approximately 25 minutes.

☐ VARIATION   Any variety of noodle can be used for this recipe, but the long, thin type is best.

☐ CHECKPOINT   The noodles should be completely dry before plunging them into the hot oil to avoid spattering.

☐

OPPOSITE

FRIED NOODLES
WITH SHRIMP

—— SERVES 4 ——

STIR-FRIED TARO AND CARROTS

*Taro is a root vegetable which is like a potato when small.
In this recipe it is cooked with carrots and flavored with hoisin
sauce to make a delicious side dish.*

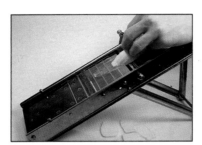

Step 1

Step 1

□ 1lb taro   □ 1 tbsp oil   □ 1¼ cups carrots, peeled and cut
into rounds   □ 2 tsps hoisin sauce   □ ½ cup beef stock
□ Salt and pepper

1. Peel the taro and cut it into thin slices. Put the thin slices back in place. Now cut the slices into thin strips. Heat the oil in a wok and stir-fry the carrots and taro for 3 minutes, shaking the wok frequently.

2. Add the hoisin sauce and the stock and continue to cook until slightly caramelized.

3. Season with salt and pepper and serve hot. The vegetables should still be quite crisp.

□ TIME   Preparation takes about 10 minutes and cooking takes approximately 15- 20 minutes.

□ COOK'S TIP   When stir-frying the taro and carrots, give them time to turn golden brown, before adding the hoisin sauce.

□ VARIATION   If you cannot buy taro, use sweet potatoes instead.

□

OPPOSITE

STIR-FRIED TARO
AND CARROTS

---— SERVES 4 ——---

CHINESE SALAD

A lovely light, fresh salad, using lots of different vegetables.
Serve chilled with a sweet and sour sauce.

Step 2

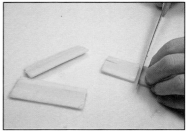

Step 2

□ 1 head lettuce, washed and dried □ 4 slices ham, cut into thin strips
□ ½ cup bamboo shoots   □ 1 cup bean sprouts, blanched in
boiling water and well drained   □ 1 carrot, cut into thin strips
□ 3 palm hearts, cut in half lengthwise and then in half again
□ ½ cucumber, cut into thin strips

FOR THE SAUCE

□ ½ tsp vinegar   □ 1 tbsp soy sauce   □ 1 tbsp oil   □ 1 tsp sugar
□ Salt and pepper

1. Shred the lettuce leaves finely and mix them with the ham. Arrange on a serving plate.

2. Prepare the bamboo shoots by slicing them first into long pieces, then cutting these pieces in half. Blanch the bamboo and drain. Sprinkle the bean sprouts over the lettuce and place the bamboo shoots over the top.

3. Garnish the salad with the other vegetables, making the dish look as attractive as possible.

4. Mix together the sauce ingredients and pour them over the prepared salad.

□ TIME   Preparation takes about 30 minutes.

□ VARIATION   Use any type of vegetable, prepared as above, to vary this salad.

□ COOK'S TIP   Cut the vegetables into very thin strips. This is important: as they are raw and therefore crunchy, some guests might have trouble with big chunks!

□

OPPOSITE

CHINESE SALAD

––––– SERVES 4 –––––

CHICKEN AND BEAN SPROUT SALAD

*Steamed chicken and bean sprouts, coated in
a refreshingly light sauce.*

Step 2

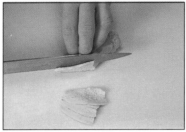
Step 3

☐ 1¾ cups bean sprouts ☐ 12oz chicken breast ☐ 1 tbsp soy sauce
☐ 2 tbsps chopped chives ☐ 1 tbsp white wine vinegar ☐ 1 tsp sugar
☐ 1 tbsp soy sauce ☐ Pinch chopped garlic ☐ 1 tbsp peanut oil
☐ ½ tsp sesame oil ☐ Salt and pepper

1. Cook the bean sprouts for 2 minutes in boiling water. Drain and refresh under cold water. Set aside to drain completely.

2. Sprinkle the chicken with 1 tsp soy sauce and cook in a Chinese steamer.

3. Once the chicken is cooked, set it aside to cool and then slice thinly.

4. Prepare the sauce by mixing together the remaining ingredients and seasoning with a little salt and pepper. Allow the sauce to stand for 20 minutes.

5. Mix together the bean sprouts and the chicken. Pour over the sauce and serve.

☐ TIME Preparation takes about 15 minutes and cooking also takes about 15 minutes.

☐ VARIATION The chicken could be cooked in stock, to which the soy sauce has been added.

☐ COOK'S TIP Mix together the sauce ingredients the day before using them. The flavors will have more time to develop fully.

☐

OPPOSITE

CHICKEN AND
BEAN SPROUT
SALAD

STEAMED ZUCCHINI FLOWERS

Try this if you can find zucchini with their flowers attached – or if you grow your own. In this delicious recipe, the flowers are stuffed, steamed and served with a light sauce.

Step 5

Step 6

☐ 1lb boned pork shoulder ☐ ½ onion ☐ 1 tbsp oil
☐ ½ tsp chopped fresh ginger root ☐ 2 tbsps soy sauce
☐ 12 small zucchini with their flowers attached ☐ 1 drop vinegar
☐ ½ tbsp sesame oil ☐ Salt and pepper

1. Cut the pork shoulder and the onion into very small cubes.

2. Heat the oil in a wok and stir-fry the ginger, pork and onion for 1 minute.

3. Stir in ½ tsp of the soy sauce and mix in well. Remove from the heat and set aside.

4. Wash the zucchini and their flowers, then steam them for 30 seconds in a Chinese steamer.

5. Refresh by plunging into cold water. Open up the flowers, by stretching them gently with your fingers.

6. Stuff the meat filling inside the flowers and down between the petals. Close the flowers again by pulling the petals back into place, to form a ball at the end of each zucchini.

7. Put them back in the steamer and cook for 4 minutes.

8. Reheat the remaining meat stuffing.

9. Mix together the remaining soy sauce, the vinegar and sesame oil. Pour this sauce over the zucchini and their flowers. Season with salt and pepper, and serve with the reheated filling.

☐ TIME   Preparation takes about 30 minutes and cooking takes approximately 20 minutes.

☐ VARIATION   As it is difficult to find zucchini with their flowers intact, you can prepare this recipe using just zucchini, sliced into rounds and steamed. Shape the rounds into "roses" and place the stuffing in the center of each "rose".

☐ COOK'S TIP   You can stuff the flowers without presteaming them, if the petals are already quite well opened.

☐

OPPOSITE

STEAMED
ZUCCHINI
FLOWERS

——— SERVES 4 ———

STIR-FRIED CHINESE CABBAGE

*Stir-fried Chinese cabbage, zucchini and peppers, flavored with
sesame oil and soy sauce.*

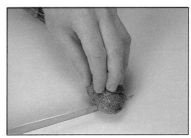

Step 1

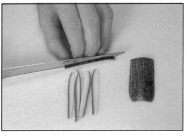

Step 1

☐ 5 cups Chinese cabbage   ☐ 2 zucchini   ☐ 2 tbsps oil
☐ 1 tsp chopped garlic   ☐ 1 tbsp chopped hot red pepper ☐ 1 tbsp soy
sauce   ☐ Salt and pepper   ☐ Few drops sesame oil

1. Shred the Chinese cabbage quite finely. Prepare the zucchini, first
topping and tailing them and then slicing down the sides, preserving a
bit of the flesh with the peel. Slice finely. Heat the oil in a wok, add the
Chinese cabbage and garlic and stir-fry for 2 minutes.

2. Add the zucchini, hot red pepper, soy sauce, salt and pepper.
Continue cooking for 3 minutes and serve hot with the sesame oil
drizzled on top.

☐   TIME   Preparation takes about 10 minutes and cooking takes
approximately 5 minutes.

☐   VARIATION   If you like hot, spicy dishes, add ¼ tsp chili sauce to
the Chinese cabbage.

☐   SERVING IDEA   Cooked in this way, the Chinese cabbage will
remain crisp. If you prefer, cook longer for a softer texture.

☐

OPPOSITE

STIR-FRIED
CHINESE
CABBAGE

—— SERVES 4 ——

STUFFED SNOW PEAS

*Steamed snow peas with a marvelous stir-fried stuffing of abalone,
scallion and ginger.*

Step 2

Step 5

□ 12 large snow peas   □ 1 tbsp oil   □ ½ tsp chopped fresh ginger root   □ 1 scallion, chopped   □ 4 pieces abalone, diced   □ 1 tbsp soy sauce   □ Salt and pepper

FOR THE SAUCE

□ 1 tbsp vinegar   □ 1 tsp sugar   □ 1 tbsp soy sauce   □ 1 tbsp chopped fresh herbs

1. Blanch the snow peas in boiling, lightly salted water. Remove from the water carefully and set aside to drain.

2. Cut the ends off each of the snow peas. Make an incision along one side of each pod. Remove the small peas from inside and reserve.

3. Heat the oil in a wok and stir-fry the ginger, scallion, abalone and the small peas for 3 minutes.

4. Stir in the soy sauce and continue cooking until the soy sauce has evaporated. Season with salt and pepper.

5. Fill each of the snow peas with the above stuffing and place them side by side in a Chinese steamer.

6. Steam them until completely heated through.

7. Mix together the sauce ingredients and serve with the hot stuffed snow peas.

□ TIME   Preparation takes about 30 minutes and cooking takes approximately 15 minutes.

□ COOK'S TIP   To help prevent the stuffing falling out of the snow peas, place them upright and side by side in the steamer.

□ CHECKPOINT   Once the snow peas have been blanched, they are quite fragile and should be handled with care.

□

OPPOSITE

STUFFED SNOW
PEAS

—— SERVES 4 ——

BEAN SPROUT SALAD

*A marvelously light and refreshing salad, which can be served
as an appetizer to many Chinese meals.*

Step 3

Step 3

□ 2 cups fresh bean sprouts   □ ½ red pepper, seeded   □ 1 carrot
□ ½ cucumber   □ 2 slices ham   □ ½ tsp chopped garlic   □ ½ tsp
chili sauce   □ 2 tbsps soy sauce   □ Salt and pepper   □ 1 tbsp oil
□ ½ tsp sugar   □ 1 drop wine vinegar   □ 1 tbsp crushed tomato
□ ½ tbsp sesame oil

1. Cook the bean sprouts in boiling water for 15 minutes. Refresh in cold water and set aside to drain.

2. Cut the pepper, carrot, cucumber and ham into thin strips.

3. In a bowl, mix together the chopped garlic, chili sauce, soy sauce, salt, pepper, oil, sugar, vinegar and crushed tomato. Stir together well to make a sauce.

4. Toss together the bean sprouts, vegetables and ham. Pour over the sauce and the sesame oil. Serve chilled.

□   TIME   Preparation takes about 20 minutes and cooking takes 15 minutes.

□   SERVING IDEA   Sprinkle with freshly chopped chives.

□   COOK'S TIP   If you have not been able to buy fresh bean sprouts, use the canned variety. Rinse them under cold running water and use directly in the salad – there is no need to cook them.

□   VARIATION   You may prefer to use the bean sprouts either raw or just lightly cooked.

□

OPPOSITE

BEAN SPROUT
SALAD

—— SERVES 4 ——

CHINESE CABBAGE SALAD
WITH MUSHROOMS

*Crisply-cooked Chinese cabbage, served
in a stir-fried mushroom sauce.*

Step 2

Step 2

Step 2

□ 12 dried black Chinese mushrooms, soaked for 15 minutes in warm water   □ ½ head Chinese cabbage, halved and shredded   □ 1 tbsp peanut oil   □ ½ clove garlic, chopped   □ 1 tbsp sugar   □ 2 tbsps soy sauce   □ ½ tbsp chopped parsley   □ Few drops sesame oil   □ Salt and pepper

1. Cook the mushrooms in boiling water for 15 minutes. Set aside to drain.

2. Prepare the Chinese cabbage by separating the leaves from the heart, chopping each leaf into narrow strips. Blanch the Chinese cabbage in boiling water for 1 minute. Refresh in cold water and leave to drain for 10 minutes.

3. Heat the oil in a wok and stir-fry the garlic, mushrooms and Chinese cabbage for 2 minutes.

4. Stir the sugar, soy sauce and parsley into the wok and cook for a further 2 minutes.

5. Season with salt and pepper, drizzle over the sesame oil and serve immediately.

□ TIME   Preparation takes about 15 minutes and cooking takes approximately 20 minutes. The Chinese cabbage must drain for 10 minutes.

□ VARIATION   If either the Chinese cabbage or the Chinese mushrooms are not available, you could replace them with ordinary varieties.

□ CHECKPOINT   The cooking time for the mushrooms can vary considerably. If they are old, they will need cooking for slightly longer. Test from time to time, for flavor and texture, cooking until tender.

□

OPPOSITE

CHINESE
CABBAGE SALAD
WITH
MUSHROOMS

---- SERVES 4 ----

VEGETABLE STIR-FRY

*A marvelous blend of Chinese vegetables and nuts, stir-fried in
a little oil and then cooked in an aromatic sauce.*

Step 1

Step 1

☐ 2 dried lotus roots, soaked overnight in water   ☐ 2 tbsps oil
☐ ¾ cup bean sprouts   ☐ ½ red pepper, seeded and finely chopped
☐ ½ green pepper, seeded and finely chopped   ☐ ½ scallion,
chopped   ☐ 4 cups Chinese cabbage, finely chopped   ☐ 1 cup
dried Chinese black mushrooms, soaked for 1 hour in warm water
☐ 1 zucchini, thinly sliced   ☐ ½ cup frozen peas   ☐ 2 tbsps cashew
nuts, roughly chopped   ☐ 1 tsp sugar   ☐ 2 tbsps soy sauce
☐ 2 cups chicken stock   ☐ Salt and pepper

1. Cook the lotus roots in boiling, lightly salted water for 20 minutes. Slice thinly.

2. Heat the oil in a wok and stir-fry, in the following order, the bean sprouts, peppers, onion, Chinese cabbage, lotus root, mushrooms, zucchini, peas and cashew nuts.

3. Stir in the sugar, soy sauce and stock.

4. Season with salt and pepper and cook for 30 minutes, stirring frequently.

5. Serve the vegetables slightly drained of the sauce.

☐ TIME   Preparation takes about 10 minutes and cooking takes approximately 35 minutes.

☐ VARIATION   Any type of nut could be used in this recipe, for example walnuts, hazelnuts or almonds.

☐ COOK'S TIP   If time permits, this recipe is even more delicious if the vegetables are stir-fried separately, each cooked vegetable being removed from the wok before continuing with the next. Finish by cooking all the vegetables together for 30 minutes in the chicken stock as above.

☐

OPPOSITE

VEGETABLE
STIR-FRY

—— SERVES 4 ——

MUSHROOM STEW

*Two types of mushrooms are cooked with oyster sauce and ginger
to make a delicious vegetable side dish.*

Step 2

Step 2

☐ 8oz dried Chinese black mushrooms, soaked for 15 minutes in warm water   ☐ 8oz dried Chinese mushrooms, soaked for 15 minutes in warm water   ☐ 1 tbsp oil   ☐ 1 tbsp each chopped garlic and fresh ginger root   ☐ 1½ cups chicken stock   ☐ 1 tbsp oyster sauce   ☐ Salt and pepper

1. Cook the mushrooms in lightly boiling water for 45 minutes. Rinse under cold water and set aside to drain.

2. Heat the oil in a wok and stir-fry the garlic and ginger. Add the mushrooms and sauté briefly. Then add the stock, followed by the oyster sauce and salt and pepper to taste. Continue cooking until the sauce is thick and coats the mushrooms.

3. Serve hot.

☐ TIME   Preparation takes 10 minutes and cooking takes approximately 1 hour.

☐ SERVING IDEA   Just before serving, sprinkle over some freshly chopped parsley.

☐ CHECKPOINT   After removing the mushrooms from the cooking water, drain through a fine strainer, so that any sand or grit is trapped in the strainer and not on the mushrooms.

☐

OPPOSITE

MUSHROOM
STEW

—— SERVES 4 ——

CHINESE CABBAGE AND CUCUMBER SALAD

Crisply-cooked Chinese cabbage marinated with cucumber in a slightly sweet sauce.

□ Scarce pound Chinese cabbage, sliced thinly   □ 1 clove garlic
□ 1 tbsp soy sauce   □ 1 tsp sugar   □ 2 tbsps sesame oil
□ Scarce pound cucumber, sliced thinly   □ Salt and pepper

Step 1

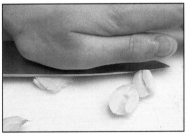
Step 1

Step 1

1. Blanch the Chinese cabbage in boiling, salted water for 1 minute. Set aside to drain. Prepare the garlic by first slicing the clove in half and removing the core. Then crush each half with the blade of a knife, and chop finely.

2. Mix together the garlic, soy sauce, sugar and sesame oil.

3. In a serving bowl, mix together the Chinese cabbage and the cucumber and season with a little salt and pepper.

4. Pour over the marinade and leave at room temperature for 2 hours.

5. Serve at room temperature.

□ TIME   Preparation takes about 20 minutes, cooking takes 1 minute and the salad needs 2 hours to marinate.

□ CHECKPOINT   Do not make the mistake of overcooking the Chinese cabbage, it should be blanched for 1 minute only, so it is tender but still crisp.

□ VARIATION   Try using light or mushroom-flavored soy sauce in this recipe.

□

OPPOSITE

CHINESE CABBAGE AND CUCUMBER SALAD

—— SERVES 4 ——

VEGETABLE CHOP SUEY

*Stir-fried vegetables, simmered in a wok with chicken stock
and soy sauce.*

Step 1

Step 1

□ 1 green pepper, seeded   □ 1 red pepper, seeded   □ 1 onion
□ 1 carrot   □ ½ cucumber   □ 1 zucchini, thickly peeled and the
central core discarded   □ 2 cloves garlic   □ 2 tbsps oil   □ 2 tsps sugar
□ 2 tbsps soy sauce   □ ½ cup chicken stock   □ Salt and pepper

1. Cut all the vegetables into thin slices. Prepare the onion by slicing it first in half, then in quarters, and finally in thin, even slices.

2. Chop the garlic very finely.

3. Heat the oil in a wok and stir-fry the peppers and garlic for 30 seconds.

4. Add the onion and the carrot and stir-fry for a further 30 seconds.

5. Add the cucumber and the zucchini, cook for a further 1 minute, stirring and shaking the wok continuously.

6. Stir in the sugar, soy sauce, chicken stock, salt and pepper, mixing together evenly. Simmer until all the ingredients are fully incorporated. Serve piping hot.

□ TIME   Preparation takes about 15 minutes and cooking takes approximately 5 minutes.

□ VARIATION   You could add blanched bean sprouts or sliced, blanched bamboo shoots to this dish.

□ COOK'S TIP   If you follow the order given above for cooking the vegetables, they will all be cooked but still slightly crisp.

□

OPPOSITE

VEGETABLE
CHOP SUEY

---SERVES 4---

SCRAMBLED EGGS WITH CRAB MEAT

Fresh crab meat with richly flavored scrambled eggs.

Step 3

Step 3

□ 3 dried Chinese mushrooms, soaked for 15 minutes in warm water   □ 1 carrot, chopped   □ 1 leek, washed and chopped   □ 1 onion, chopped   □ 1 large crab   □ 8 eggs, beaten   □ Few drops sesame oil   □ 1 tsp sake   □ 1 tbsp soy sauce   □ Salt and pepper

---

1. Cook the mushrooms in boiling, salted water for 15 minutes. Rinse in fresh water and set aside to drain.

2. Cook the crab for 15 minutes in a vegetable stock made from 8 cups water, the carrot, leek and onion. Remove the crab and set aside to cool.

3. When the crab is cool enough to handle, break off the pinchers, break open the back and all the joints and remove the meat.

4. In a large bowl, mix together the eggs, sliced mushrooms, sesame oil, sake, soy sauce and the crab meat. Season with salt and pepper.

5. Cook by stirring the eggs over a very gentle heat in a nonstick frying pan. The eggs will thicken slowly. When cooked to your liking, serve immediately.

□ TIME   Preparation takes about 30 minutes, as extracting the crab meat takes quite a while, and cooking takes approximately 30 minutes.

□ TIMESAVER   The use of canned crab meat cuts the preparation and cooking time considerably.

□ WATCHPOINT   Do not cook the eggs too quickly, or they will become hard and dry.

□

OPPOSITE

SCRAMBLED
EGGS WITH
CRAB MEAT

SERVES 4

SCRAMBLED EGGS WITH SHRIMP

Fish-flavored scrambled eggs, cooked with shrimp.

Step 2

Step 2

□ 12 shrimp, peeled   □ 8 eggs, beaten   □ ½ stick celery, cut into small dice   □ 1 scallion, chopped   □ 1 tsp fish sauce   □ Salt and pepper

1. Cut the shrimp into small pieces.

2. Stir the shrimp into the eggs and add the celery, scallion and fish sauce.

3. Season with a little salt and pepper.

4. Cook by stirring over a gentle heat. When cooked to your liking, serve immediately.

□ TIME   Preparation takes about 10 minutes and cooking takes approximately 10 minutes.

□ SERVING IDEA   Serve with lightly steamed shrimp.

□ CHECKPOINT   The fish sauce is very salty. Only add more salt after cooking, if necessary.

□

OPPOSITE

SCRAMBLED
EGGS WITH
SHRIMP

————— SERVES 4 —————

BROCCOLI WITH OYSTERS

*Broccoli tips are cooked in a marvelous ginger sauce and
served with lightly poached oysters.*

Step 1

Step 1

☐ 1½lbs broccoli   ☐ 8 large oysters   ☐ 1¼ cups pint fish stock
☐ 1 tsp chopped fresh ginger root   ☐ 1 sprig fresh thyme   ☐ 1 tbsp
oyster sauce   ☐ 1 tsp cornstarch, combined with a little water
☐ Salt and pepper

---

1. Choose fresh, green broccoli. Cut off the tough stalks, trim the
broccoli and rinse well. Precook the broccoli in boiling, lightly salted
water, until tender but still crisp. Refresh by plunging into cold water
and set aside to drain.

2. Open the oyster shells, cut out and set aside the oyster, discarding
both juice and shell.

3. Heat the fish stock and add the ginger, thyme and precooked
broccoli. Cook, covered, for 5 minutes.

4. Remove the broccoli and add the oysters in their place. Poach these
for 1 minute, then remove and place on a hot serving plate.

5. Stir the oyster sauce into the fish stock, remove the thyme and
thicken the sauce by stirring in the cornstarch. Adjust the seasoning as
necessary.

6. Serve the oysters surrounded by the broccoli and accompanied with
the sauce.

☐ TIME   Preparation takes about 15 minutes and cooking takes
approximately 25 minutes.

☐ SERVING IDEA   If your guests are using chopsticks, serve the
sauce separately so guests can dip the oysters and the broccoli into it
using their own chopsticks.

☐ COOK'S TIP   The sauce may be thick enough by itself without
using the cornstarch, or it could be thickened by reduction.

☐

OPPOSITE

BROCCOLI WITH
OYSTERS

SERVES 4

CHINESE CABBAGE WITH OYSTERS

Chinese cabbage is here cooked in fish stock, with oysters and bacon.

Step 1

Step 1

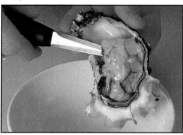

Step 1

☐ 12 large oysters   ☐ 5 cups Chinese cabbage   ☐ 1 tbsp oil
☐ 1 cup bacon, diced   ☐ ¼ cup fish stock   ☐ Salt and pepper

1. Use large oysters if possible. If you have to use the smaller variety, increase the number accordingly. Open the oysters, taking care to protect your hand by wrapping a kitchen towel around the oyster. Cut the oysters away from the shell, reserving the oysters and their juice, but discarding the shells.

2. Shred the Chinese cabbage.

3. Heat the oil in a wok and stir-fry the bacon.

4. Stir the Chinese cabbage into the wok and add the fish stock. Check the seasoning, adding salt and pepper to taste. Continue until the Chinese cabbage is cooked to your liking.

5. Place the oysters and their juice on top of the Chinese cabbage and poach for approximately 2 minutes. 6. Remove the oysters and place on a hot serving plate.

7. Serve immediately, accompanied with the cooked Chinese cabbage.

☐ TIME   Preparation takes about 25 minutes and cooking takes approximately 10 minutes.

☐ CHECKPOINT   Taste the sauce before adding salt, as the bacon and oysters are naturally rather salty.

☐ COOK'S TIP   If you prefer your oysters a little more cooked, increase the cooking time by another 2 minutes. Do not overcook them, or they become chewy.

☐

OPPOSITE

CHINESE
CABBAGE WITH
OYSTERS

SERVES 4

FRIED CHINESE RAVIOLI
WITH SALMON

Wonton dough squares filled with a salmon stuffing and deep-fried.

Step 4

Step 5

Step 5

☐ 8oz fresh salmon, boned, filleted and finely ground   ☐ 1 tbsp chopped fresh chives   ☐ 1 squeeze lemon juice   ☐ 1 egg, beaten   ☐ 24 wonton wrappers   ☐ Salt and pepper   ☐ Oil for deep-frying

---

1. Mix the salmon with the chives, lemon juice, salt and pepper.

2. Spread out 12 wonton wrappers and divide the stuffing evenly between them, placing it in the center of each wrapper.

3. Brush the beaten egg around the edges of the stuffing and top with the remaining 12 wrappers.

4. Cut each one into the desired shape and seal the edges firmly by pinching with your fingers or pushing down with a fork. Set aside to rest for 15 minutes.

5. Heat the oil to 340°F. Cook the ravioli a few at a time in the hot oil. Remove when cooked and drain them on paper towels.

6. Season with salt and pepper and serve immediately.

☐ TIME   Preparation takes about 20 minutes and cooking, depending on the number of batches, takes 8-15 minutes.

☐ SERVING IDEA   Serve with slices of salmon, heated through in a frying pan, and chopped, fried onions.

☐ COOK'S TIP   If you use a food processor to grind the fish, be careful not to reduce it to a purée; processing for a second or two is all that is necessary.

☐

OPPOSITE

FRIED CHINESE
RAVIOLI WITH
SALMON

—— SERVES 4 ——

SHRIMP WITH VEGETABLES

Quick-fried shrimp, served with stir-fried Chinese vegetables.

Step 1

Step 1

□ ½ cucumber   □ 1 cup bean sprouts   □ 8 dried Chinese black mushrooms, soaked in warm water for 15 minutes   □ 2 tbsps peanut oil   □ 1 clove garlic, chopped   □ 1 tsp sugar   □ 1 tsp oyster sauce   □ 1 tsp wine vinegar   □ Salt and pepper   □ 1 tsp oil   □ 20 shrimp, peeled and deveined*   □ 2 tbsps cornstarch   □ 1 tbsp soy sauce   □ 1 tbsp sesame oil

1. Peel the cucumber all around with a sharp knife. Slice into julienne.

2. Rinse and drain the bean sprouts.

3. Drain the mushrooms and cook in boiling, salted water for 15 minutes. Rinse and set aside to drain.

4. Heat the peanut oil in a wok and stir-fry the garlic, bean sprouts and mushrooms for 1 minute.

5. Add the cucumber, sugar, oyster sauce, vinegar and salt and pepper, and cook for 2 minutes, stirring continuously.

6. Heat the oil in a frying pan. Toss the shrimp in the cornstarch and fry them until cooked through.

7. Transfer the vegetables to a serving platter. Top with the fried shrimp. Sprinkle with soy sauce and the sesame oil just before serving.

□ TIME   Preparation takes about 15-20 minutes, reconstituting the mushrooms 15 minutes and cooking takes approximately 10 minutes.

□ *COOK'S TIP   It is advisable to devein the shrimp by removing the black thread from the indentation along the back of the prawn with a small, sharp knife.

□ CHECKPOINT   Before serving, the vegetables should have caramelized slightly.

□

OPPOSITE

SHRIMP WITH
VEGETABLES

SHRIMP WITH ONIONS

*Diced onions are first marinated and then stir-fried with shrimp
and served in a soy-flavored sauce.*

Step 1

□ 2 large onions, diced   □ 2 tbsps soy sauce   □ 2 tsps sugar
□ 2 tbsps oil   □ 16 shrimp, peeled and deveined   □ ½ cup fish stock
□ Salt and pepper

1. Combine the diced onion with the soy sauce and the sugar. Marinate for 15 minutes, stirring frequently.

2. Heat the oil and stir-fry the shrimp. Remove when cooked, but keep warm.

3. Add the onions and the marinade to the wok and stir-fry gently for 5 minutes. Season with salt and pepper to taste.

4. Add the stock to the onions, and continue cooking until the liquid has reduced. Serve the onions topped with the shrimp.

□ TIME   Preparation takes 10 minutes, marinating 15 minutes and cooking takes approximately 20 minutes.

□ COOK'S TIP   Keep the fried shrimp in a warm oven or reheat for 1 minute in a microwave oven before serving.

□ CHECKPOINT   In Step 4, the liquid should be allowed to reduce considerably.

□

OPPOSITE

SHRIMP WITH
ONIONS

CRAB WITH BAMBOO SHOOTS

*Cooked crab, stir-fried with bamboo shoots and served
in a hot, spicy sauce.*

Step 1

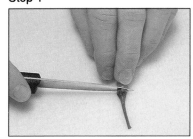

Step 1

Step 1

☐ 1 fresh hot chili pepper ☐ 2 medium-sized crabs, precooked for approximately 15 minutes in fish stock ☐ 1 cup bamboo shoots ☐ 1 tbsp oil ☐ 4 slices fresh ginger root ☐ ½ onion, chopped ☐ 1 tsp vinegar ☐ 1 tsp sugar ☐ 1 cup fish stock ☐ 1 tsp cornstarch, blended with a little water ☐ Salt and pepper ☐ 1 tbsp chopped fresh chives

1. Prepare the fresh hot chili pepper. Cut off the stalk end, slice the pepper in half and remove the pith and seeds from the center. Chop the pepper as finely as possible.

2. Remove all the flesh from the cooked crab and set aside.

3. Cut the bamboo shoots into thin slices and blanch them in boiling, lightly salted water.

4. Heat the oil in a wok and stir-fry the ginger, onion and bamboo shoots for 1 minute.

5. Stir in the crab and as much of the chili pepper as you like, and fry for 1 minute.

6. Stir in the vinegar, sugar and fish stock and cook for 5 minutes over a gentle heat. Thicken by adding the cornstarch, stirring continuously.

7. Season to taste with salt and pepper, sprinkle with chopped chives and serve.

☐ TIME   Preparation takes about 20 minutes and cooking takes approximately 10 minutes.

☐ VARIATION   If fresh crab is not available, use 2 medium-sized cans of crab, rinsed and well-drained.

☐ CHECKPOINT   Add the fresh hot chili pepper gradually, tasting after each addition to check the hotness of the dish.

☐

OPPOSITE

CRAB WITH BAMBOO SHOOTS

—— SERVES 4 ——

SWEET AND SOUR SHELLFISH

*Clams cooked in a light, sweet sauce and served
with matchstick vegetables.*

Step 2

Step 5

□ 20 clams, rinsed in plenty of running water   □ 100ml/4 fl oz
Chinese wine   □ 1 tbsp oil   □ 1 tsp each finely chopped garlic and
fresh ginger root   □ ½ red pepper, seeded and cut into thin
matchsticks   □ ½ green pepper, seeded and cut into thin matchsticks
□ ¼ cucumber, peeled and cut into thin matchsticks   □ 1 tbsp soy sauce
□ 2 tbsps pineapple or orange juice   □ 1 tsp wine vinegar
□ Salt and pepper

1. Place the clams in a wide-based saucepan, pour in the wine, cover, and place over a high heat to open the shells, which should take approximately 3-5 minutes.

2. Remove the clams from their shells. Drain the cooking liquid through a very fine sieve and reserve. Keep the shells to one side.

3. Heat the oil in a wok and stir-fry the ginger, garlic, vegetables and clams for 2 minutes.

4. Stir in the soy sauce, 4 tbsps of the reserved cooking liquid, the pineapple or orange juice, and the vinegar. Season with salt and pepper to taste. Cook until the sauce is slightly reduced and the clams are tender.

5. Replace the cooked clams, with the sauce, in the reserved shells. Cook in a hot oven for 2 minutes and serve immediately.

□ TIME   Preparation takes about 10 minutes and cooking takes approximately 25 minutes.
□ VARIATION   Any shellfish could be used instead of the clams.
□ CHECKPOINT   Clams are often tough and rubbery and need to be cooked long enough to tenderize them.

□

OPPOSITE

SWEET AND SOUR
SHELLFISH

— SERVES 4 —

SHELLFISH IN EGG NOODLE NESTS

Fried egg noodle nests are filled with mussels and cockles in an oyster sauce and garnished with matchstick vegetables.

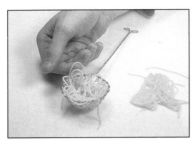

Step 5

Step 5

Step 6

☐ 5oz Chinese egg noodles ☐ 24 mussels, washed and thoroughly rinsed to remove sand ☐ 6oz cockles, washed and thoroughly rinsed to remove sand ☐ 1 cup Chinese wine ☐ 1 small zucchini ☐ Oil for deep-frying ☐ 1 tbsp oil ☐ ½ tsp each finely chopped fresh ginger root and garlic ☐ 2 leaves Chinese cabbage, shredded ☐ ½ tbsp soy sauce ☐ ½ tbsp oyster sauce ☐ Salt and pepper

1. Cook the egg noodles in boiling, lightly salted water. Rinse under cold water and set aside to drain.

2. Cook the mussels and cockles with the wine in a large covered saucepan for about 3-5 minutes, until the shells have opened.

3. Remove the mussels and cockles from their shells.

4. Peel the zucchini and slice the peel into thin matchsticks. Discard the flesh and seeds.

5. Heat the oil in a deep-fat fryer to 350°F. Make the noodle nests by placing a few noodles on the inside of a basket fryer or a metal draining spoon. Clamp the noodles in place with a second basket or draining spoon.

6. Plunge each nest into the hot oil and cook for 1-2 minutes until golden brown and crisp. Remove the nest and drain it on paper towels. Repeat the process with the remaining noodles.

7. Heat the 1 tbsp oil in a wok and stir-fry the garlic, ginger, cockles, mussels and Chinese cabbage for 1 minute.

8. Stir in the soy and oyster sauces and season to taste with salt and pepper. Allow the liquid to reduce slightly. Divide the mixture evenly between the fried egg noodle nests.

☐ TIME   Preparation takes about 40 minutes and cooking takes approximately 50 minutes.

☐ SERVING IDEA   Serve on a bed of shredded lettuce.

☐ COOK'S TIP   Once the nests are cooked, tap the baskets or metal spoons on a plate or table top to dislodge them.

☐

OPPOSITE

SHELLFISH IN EGG NOODLE NESTS

—— SERVES 4 ——

TROUT IN OYSTER SAUCE

Steamed trout fillets served on a bed of vegetables in sweet and sour sauce.

Step 1

Step 1

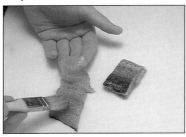

Step 1

☐ 2 trout ☐ 2 tbsps oyster sauce ☐ ½ cup bamboo shoots, cut in matchsticks ☐ 1 tbsp oil ☐ 1 tsp each chopped fresh ginger root and garlic ☐ ½ green pepper, finely chopped ☐ ½ red pepper, finely chopped ☐ ½ onion, finely chopped ☐ 1 tsp sugar ☐ 1 tsp vinegar ☐ Juice of ½ orange ☐ 2 tbsps soy sauce ☐ 1 cup fish stock ☐ 1 tsp cornstarch, combined with a little water ☐ Salt and pepper

1. Fillet the trout, then cut the fillets into several pieces.

2. Season the pieces with salt and pepper, and brush each one with oyster sauce. Then stack in pairs and set aside.

3. Blanch the bamboo shoots and rinse. Allow to drain.

4. Heat the oil in a wok and stir-fry the ginger, garlic, peppers, onion and bamboo shoots.

5. Add the sugar, vinegar, orange juice, soy sauce and fish stock and cook together for 3 minutes.

6. Season to taste, then add the cornstarch, stirring continuously until thickened.

7. Steam the trout pieces separately for approximately 3 minutes, according to their thickness. Serve the fish on a bed of the vegetables in sauce.

☐ TIME   Preparation takes about 30 minutes and cooking takes 15 minutes.

☐ COOK'S TIP   Either freshwater or sea trout can be used in this dish, although sea trout is preferable.

☐ CHECKPOINT   The trout can be steamed whole and divided up just before serving. The cooking time should then be varied accordingly.

☐

OPPOSITE

TROUT IN
OYSTER SAUCE

───── SERVES 4 ─────

───── SERVES 4 ─────

BROILED SEA SCALLOPS
WITH ASPARAGUS

*Sea scallops accompanied with fresh asparagus and served with
a sweet and sour dipping sauce.*

Step 1

Step 1

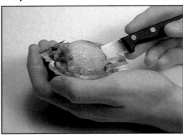
Step 1

□ 16 sea scallops   □ 16 stalks green asparagus   □ 1 tbsp oil

DIPPING SAUCE

□ 1 tbsp soy sauce   □ 2 tsps sugar   □ ½ scallion, finely chopped
□ 1 tbsp oil   □ 1 tsp wine vinegar   □ Salt and pepper

1. With the point of a sharp knife, pry open the scallops, and extract the scallop and the coral. Rinse well and allow to dry on a kitchen towel.

2. Boil the asparagus in salted water until tender, and refresh in cold water. Drain and halve lengthwise.

3. Make the dipping sauce, by combining the soy sauce, sugar, scallion, oil, vinegar and salt and pepper to taste.

4. Brush the scallops and corals with oil and season with salt and pepper.

5. Preheat the broiler or oil a frying pan, and quickly broil or sauté the scallops, turning them very gently. Cook for 1 minute on each side.

6. Serve the scallops with the asparagus to dip in the sauce.

□ TIME   Preparation takes 45 minutes and cooking takes 15 minutes.

□ COOK'S TIP   If possible, make the dipping sauce a day in advance, to allow the flavors to develop more fully.

□ CHECKPOINT   The broiling or frying of the scallops is a delicate operation which must be carried out quickly and gently, to avoid damaging the central body of the scallop.

□

OPPOSITE

BROILED SEA
SCALLOPS WITH
ASPARAGUS

——— SERVES 4 ———

STIR-FRIED LOBSTER WITH GINGER

Fresh lobster sautéed with zucchini in a pungent fish sauce.

☐ 2 lobsters, each 12oz in weight ☐ 1 tbsp vinegar ☐ 1 zucchini
☐ 1 tbsp oil ☐ 2 tsps chopped fresh ginger root ☐ 1 tbsp oyster sauce
☐ ¼ cup fish stock ☐ 1 tsp cornstarch, combined with a little water
☐ Salt and pepper

Step 4

Step 5

1. To cook the lobsters, bring a large pan of salted water to the boil, and add the vinegar. Drop in the lobsters and boil for 15 minutes. Drain, allow to cool and shell the lobsters.

2. Slice the lobster meat into serving-sized pieces.

3. Slice the zucchini thinly.

4. In a wok, heat the oil, and stir-fry the ginger. Add the zucchini and cook until tender but still crisp. Add the lobster and heat through.

5. Pour in the oyster sauce and the fish stock, season with salt and pepper to taste and allow to reduce.

6. Thicken the sauce with the cornstarch paste, stirring continuously.

☐ TIME   Preparation takes about 45 minutes, including cooking the lobsters, and cooking takes 15 minutes.

☐ COOK'S TIP   Crawfish may be used instead of lobster.

☐ CHECKPOINT   Use a nutcracker to break open the lobster claws.

☐

OPPOSITE

STIR-FRIED LOBSTER WITH GINGER

SERVES 4

CHINESE RAW FISH

Step 1

Step 2

☐ 8oz firm-fleshed fish fillets, e.g. haddock or cod   ☐ 8oz sea bass
☐ 1 tsp each finely chopped fresh ginger root and garlic
☐ 1 tsp finely chopped shallot   ☐ Juice of 1 lemon
☐ 10 coriander seeds, crushed   ☐ Few drops sesame oil   ☐ Salt and
pepper   ☐ 1 tbsp chopped fresh chives

1. Slice the fish very thinly, spread the slices out on a plate, and sprinkle with the chopped ginger, garlic and shallot.

2. Squeeze on the lemon juice and sprinkle with the crushed coriander seeds.

3. Drizzle on the sesame oil.

4. Allow to marinate for 30 minutes.

5. Season with salt and pepper to taste, garnish with the chopped chives and serve.

☐   TIME   Preparation takes about 45 minutes.

☐   COOK'S TIP   Any fresh fish is suitable for this recipe.

☐   CHECKPOINT   Do not allow the fish to marinate for more than 30 minutes, as it will become "overcooked" by the acidity in the lemon juice.

☐

OPPOSITE

CHINESE RAW
FISH

---------- SERVES 4 ----------

BREAM IN SWEET
AND SOUR SAUCE

*Steamed fillet of sea bream, accompanied by a spicy
sweet and sour sauce.*

Step 1

Step 5

☐ 1 sea bream, approximately 2lbs   ☐ ½ red pepper, seeded
☐ ½ green pepper, seeded   ☐ ¼ cucumber   ☐ 1 tsp each finely
chopped fresh ginger root and garlic   ☐ 2 scallions, finely chopped
☐ 1 tbsp oil   ☐ ¼ small fresh hot chili pepper, seeded   ☐ 3 tbsps
pineapple juice   ☐ 2 tbsps crushed tomato   ☐ ½ cup fish stock
☐ 1 tsp cornstarch, combined with a little water   ☐ 1 tbsp vinegar
☐ Salt and pepper   ☐ 1 sheet dried seaweed (optional)
☐ 1 tbsp chopped fresh chives

1. Scale and gut the bream. Fillet the fish, removing any bones, and cut the fillets into medium-sized pieces.

2. Cut the red and green peppers and the cucumber into fine julienne.

3. In a wok, heat the oil, and sauté for 1 minute the vegetables, ginger, garlic, scallion and the ¼ hot chili pepper. Add the pineapple juice, the crushed tomato and the fish stock. Simmer over a low heat for 2 minutes.

4. Thicken the sauce with the cornstarch paste, stirring continuously. Discard the hot chili pepper, add the vinegar and season with salt and pepper to taste.

5. Steam the bream over water containing strips of the dried seaweed, if using.

6. Serve the fish accompanied with the sweet and sour sauce and sprinkled with the chopped chives.

☐ TIME   Preparation takes about 30 minutes and cooking takes about 15 minutes.

☐ COOK'S TIP   Steaming the bream over water containing dried seaweed enhances the flavor of the fish.

☐ CHECKPOINT   As they cook, the pieces of bream will curl up.

☐ BUYING GUIDE   If you cannot obtain sea bream, substitute the same weight of red snapper.

☐

OPPOSITE

BREAM IN SWEET
AND SOUR
SAUCE

—— SERVES 4 ——

SEA BASS IN FIVE-SPICE SAUCE

Fillets of sea bass are marinated and then quickly sautéed.

Step 1

Step 3

☐ 1lb sea bass fillets ☐ 1 tbsp fish sauce ☐ 1 tbsp Shaohsing wine ☐ 1 tsp oyster sauce ☐ ½ tsp finely chopped fresh ginger root ☐ 2 shallots, chopped ☐ 2 tsps five-spice powder ☐ 1 tbsp oil ☐ Salt and pepper

1. Slice the sea bass fillets evenly. Arrange the slices on a plate.

2. In a bowl, combine the fish sauce, Shaohsing wine, oyster sauce, chopped ginger, shallots and five-spice powder.

3. Season the fish with salt and pepper and leave to marinate in the above mixture for 1 hour.

4. In a frying pan, heat the oil; drain the fish fillets and fry the fish briefly for 30 seconds on each side. Serve immediately.

☐ TIME   Preparation takes about 10 minutes, marinating takes 1 hour and cooking takes 1 minute.

☐ COOK'S TIP   The fish is generally served without a separate sauce, but if a sauce is preferred, mix together 1 tbsp fish sauce, 1 tbsp water, 1 tbsp soy sauce, 1 tsp sugar and ½ tsp five-spice powder.

☐

OPPOSITE

SEA BASS IN FIVE-SPICE SAUCE

---- SERVES 4 ----

BREADED SHRIMP WITH FRESH TOMATO SALAD

Pan-fried, breaded shrimp served with a fresh tomato and ginger salad.

Step 5

Step 5

☐ 5 ripe tomatoes   ☐ 1 tsp finely chopped fresh ginger root   ☐ 1 tbsp finely chopped fresh chives   ☐ 24 fresh shrimp   ☐ 2 tbsps oil   ☐ 2 tbsps all-purpose flour   ☐ 2 eggs, beaten   ☐ 4 tbsps fine bread crumbs   ☐ Salt and pepper

1. Bring a saucepan of water to the boil, and immerse the tomatoes in it for 15 seconds. Rinse immediately in cold water and allow to cool. Peel, seed and finely chop the tomatoes.

2. Mix the ginger and chives together thoroughly with the tomatoes. Season and allow to marinate for 2 hours in the refrigerator.

3. Shell the shrimp, leaving the tails intact.

4. Heat the oil in a frying pan.

5. Dredge the shrimp in the flour, then dip them in the beaten egg, and finally coat them in the breadcrumbs. Fry until golden.

6. Serve the fried shrimp on a bed of chilled tomato salad, garnished with chopped chives, if desired.

☐ TIME   Preparation takes about 10 minutes, marinating takes 2 hours and cooking takes about 10 minutes.

☐ COOK'S TIP   Prepare the tomato salad a day in advance, so that the flavor of the ginger has time to develop fully.

☐

OPPOSITE

BREADED SHRIMP WITH FRESH TOMATO SALAD

SERVES 4

CRAB ROLLS

*Chinese pancakes are first filled with a delicious crab mixture, then
rolled up and quick-fried until crisp and golden.*

Step 1

Step 1

Step 1

BATTER

□ ¾ cup all-purpose flour, sifted   □ Salt   □ 4 eggs, beaten
□ ½ cup water

FILLING

□ 1lb crab meat   □ 1 egg, beaten   □ 1 tbsp chopped scallion
□ 1 tbsp chopped fresh chives   □ Salt and pepper   □ 1 tsp soy sauce
□ ¼ cup oil   □ 1 egg, beaten

1. Make the pancake batter first, by mixing together the flour, a large pinch of salt, the four eggs and the water. Beat the mixture well and set aside to rest for 10 minutes.

2. Mix together the crab meat, one single beaten egg, the scallion, chives, salt and pepper to taste, and soy sauce.

3. Heat 1 tbsp of the oil in a wok and stir-fry the crab filling. Once cooked, remove the mixture from the wok and allow it to cool.

4. Use the batter to make pancakes. Cook them one at a time in a frying pan, using as little oil as necessary, until lightly browned on each side. Keep the cooked pancakes covered and warm while cooking the others.

5. Place a little of the crab mixture in the center of each pancake. Roll them up as for spring rolls and use the one remaining egg to seal the ends and the sides. Set the rolls aside for a few minutes.

6. Heat the remaining oil in a frying pan and fry the rolls gently until crisp, then remove them from the oil, drain on paper towels and serve immediately.

□ TIME   Preparation takes about 15 minutes and cooking takes approximately 30 minutes.

□ SERVING IDEA   A tasty sauce to accompany these rolls can be made by mixing together 1 tbsp fish sauce, ½ cup fish stock, 2 tsps sugar and 1 tsp chopped fresh ginger root.

□ COOK'S TIP   Cook the pancakes in a nonstick frying pan to avoid using oil. If using a traditional pan, use as little oil as necessary.

□

OPPOSITE

CRAB ROLLS

----- SERVES 4 -----

TROUT FILLETS WITH GINGER AND SCALLION

Steamed trout fillets cooked with scallion and ginger and served with a slightly sweet sauce.

Step 1

Step 1

☐ 4 sea trout fillets ☐ Salt and pepper ☐ 1 scallion, chopped
☐ 1 tsp chopped fresh ginger root ☐ ½ cup vinegar ☐ ½ cup soy sauce
☐ 3 tsps sugar ☐ ½ cup fish stock

1. Season the trout fillets with salt and pepper. Lay them in a steam basket and sprinkle over the scallion and the ginger. Set aside.

2. In a saucepan, mix together the vinegar, soy sauce, sugar and fish stock. Place over a high heat and allow to reduce and thicken.

3. While the sauce is cooking, steam the trout for about 5 minutes, until cooked.

4. Serve the fish fillets topped with the sauce.

☐ TIME   Preparation takes about 5 minutes and cooking takes approximately 15 minutes.

☐ SERVING IDEA   The vinegar sauce can be served hot or cold.

☐ CHECKPOINT   Do not overcook the trout fillets. If they are quite thin, 3 minutes steaming may be sufficient.

☐

OPPOSITE

TROUT FILLETS
WITH GINGER
AND SCALLION

—— SERVES 4 ——

MONKFISH WITH ONIONS AND VINEGAR SAUCE

Chunks of monkfish are cooked and served in an onion and vinegar sauce.

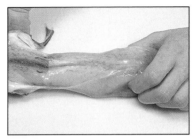

Step 1

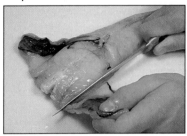

Step 3

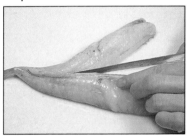

Step 3

□ 1 large monkfish, cleaned   □ 2 tbsps oil   □ 2 large onions, finely sliced   □ 2 tbsps white wine vinegar   □ 2 tsps sugar   □ 1 tbsp soy sauce   □ 1½ cups fish stock   □ ½ tsp chopped fresh ginger root   □ Salt and pepper   □ 1 tsp cornstarch, combined with a little water

1. Prepare the fish by pulling off the skin in one piece, easing the skin from around the head and then pulling it down gently, but firmly, towards the tail.

2. Cut off the the head and tail, and clean the inside thoroughly.

3. Fillet the fish by sliding a sharp knife between the flesh and the central bones on each side. Cut both fillets in half.

4. Heat the oil in a wok, stir-fry the onions gently until soft and then ease them up the sides of the wok.

5. Add the fish fillets to the wok, stir-fry for 1 minute, then push the onions back into the wok with the fish. Deglaze the pan with the vinegar and stir in the sugar, soy sauce, fish stock and ginger.

6. Season with salt and pepper to taste, stir well, cover and cook for 7 minutes over a gentle heat.

7. Remove the fish, cut it into thin slices and keep on a hot plate.

8. Add the cornstarch to the sauce and stir continuously, until the sauce thickens.

9. Place the onions and their sauce on a hot serving plate. Place the sliced fish on top and serve immediately.

□ TIME   Preparation takes about 15 minutes and cooking takes approximately 15 minutes.

□ VARIATION   When scallions are in season, use about five instead of the onions. They should be shredded finely and cooked as above.

□ CHECKPOINT   Cook the onions over a gentle heat, as they should be soft and transparent, not brown. Ease them up the sides of the wok as soon as they are cooked.

□

OPPOSITE

MONKFISH WITH
ONIONS AND
VINEGAR SAUCE

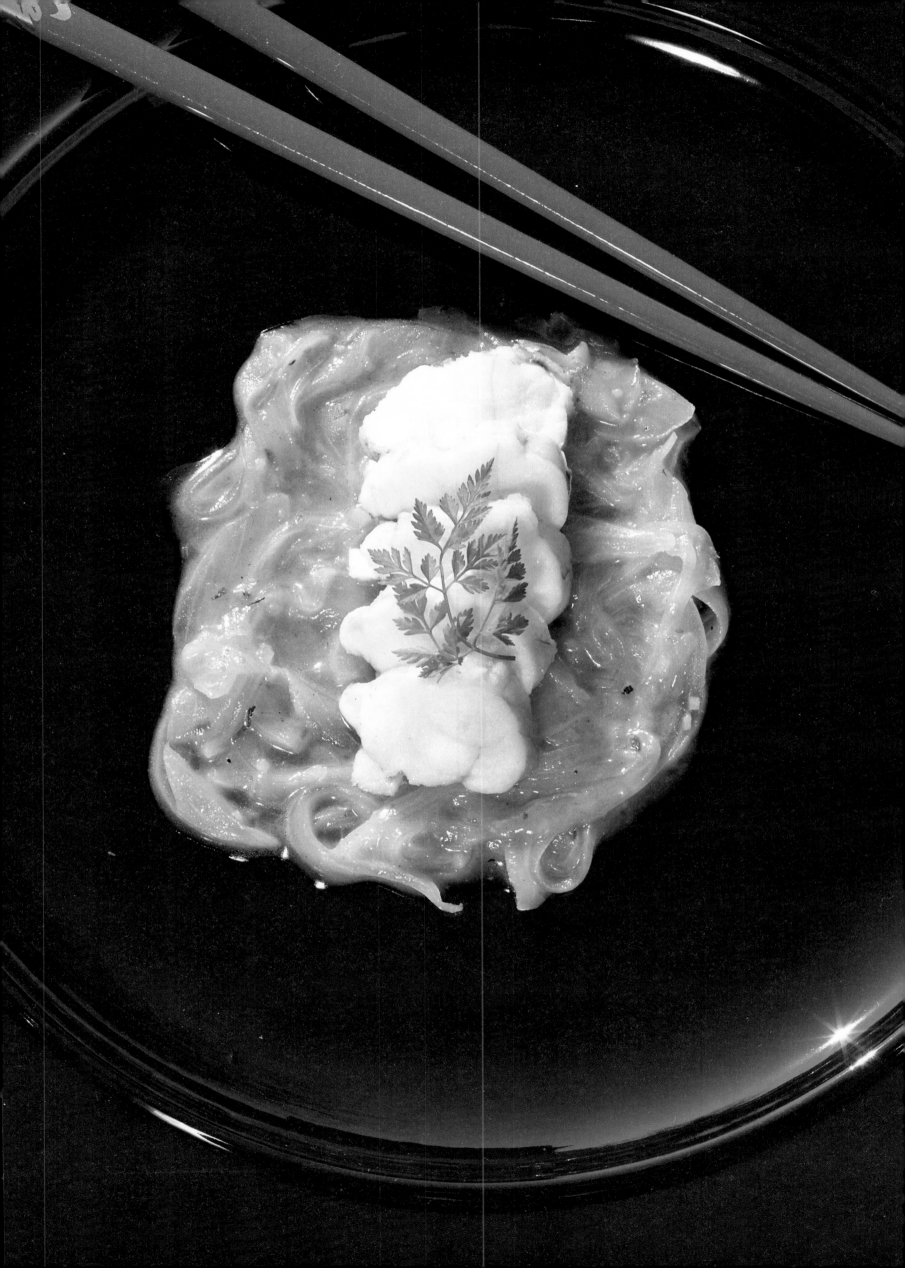

SERVES 4

WHITING FRITTERS WITH
COLD FISH SAUCE

Step 1

Step 2

□ 1½ cups all-purpose flour, sifted   □ 1 tsp baking powder
□ ½ cup water   □ 1 egg, beaten   □ 1 tsp oil   □ 1lb whiting fillets
□ Salt and pepper   □ Oil for deep-frying

FOR THE SAUCE

□ 1 tbsp fish sauce   □ 1 tbsp soy sauce   □ 1 tbsp fish stock
□ Few leaves fresh mint, finely chopped

1. Make the batter by mixing together the sifted flour and the baking powder.

2. Mix in the water, followed by the egg.

3. Add the oil and a good pinch of salt and beat all the ingredients together well. Set the batter aside to rest for a few minutes.

4. Season the whiting fillets with salt and pepper and cut them into small strips.

5. Heat the oil for deep-frying. Dip the whiting strips into the batter and fry them in the hot oil until crisp and golden.

6. Remove the fritters and drain them on paper towels. Keep hot.

7. Meanwhile, mix together the sauce ingredients and serve with the hot whiting fritters.

□ TIME   Preparation takes about 15 minutes and cooking takes approximately 20 minutes, as you will need to fry the fritters in several batches.

□ VARIATION   If you do not have the sauce ingredients, the fritters are delicious with a little lemon juice.

□ COOK'S TIP   Make the sauce a few hours in advance. This gives the flavor of the mint time to develop.

□

OPPOSITE

WHITING
FRITTERS WITH
COLD FISH SAUCE

BREAM WITH PINEAPPLE

Steamed bream fillets, served with a stir-fried pineapple sauce.

Step 1

Step 1

☐ 1 large bream ☐ 2 tbsps oil ☐ ½ tsp chopped garlic ☐ 4 slices of canned pineapple, cut into small pieces ☐ 1 tbsp soy sauce ☐ ¼ cup pineapple syrup, from the can ☐ 1¼ cups fish stock ☐ 1 tsp cornstarch, combined with a little water ☐ Salt and pepper

1. Cut the fins off the fish. Fillet the fish, using a sharp knife to cut between the flesh and the bones on each side. Discard the head, tail and bones.

2. Heat 1 tbsp of the oil in a wok and stir-fry the garlic and the pineapple pieces.

3. Pour off any excess fat and add the soy sauce, pineapple syrup and fish stock. Allow the sauce to reduce a little and then add the cornstarch, stirring continuously until the sauce thickens. Remove the sauce and keep warm.

4. Heat the remaining oil in the cleaned wok and stir-fry the pieces of fish, seasoning them with salt and pepper. Shake the wok frequently to cook the fish evenly.

5. Serve the fish hot, topped with the sauce.

☐ TIME   Preparation takes about 15 minutes and cooking takes approximately 15 minutes.

☐ VARIATION   You could vary this recipe by substituting the same proportion of orange for the pineapple.

☐ COOK'S TIP   Begin cooking the fish pieces skin side down and allow them to become quite crisp before turning them to cook the second side.

☐ BUYING GUIDE   If you cannot obtain bream, substitute red snapper.

☐

OPPOSITE

BREAM WITH
PINEAPPLE

—— SERVES 4 ——

DEEP-FRIED STICKY RICE
WITH PRAWNS

*Fried glutinous rice with king prawns, served in
a sweet and sour sauce.*

Step 6

Step 6

☐ 8oz glutinous rice   ☐ 20 fresh king prawns   ☐ 1 tbsp oil
☐ 1 tsp finely chopped garlic   ☐ 1 tsp finely chopped fresh ginger root
☐ 1 small green pepper, seeded and finely chopped   ☐ 1 small red
pepper, seeded and finely chopped   ☐ ½ cucumber, finely chopped
☐ 1 onion, finely chopped   ☐ 1 tbsp soy sauce   ☐ Juice of 1 orange
☐ ½ tbsp vinegar   ☐ 1 tsp sugar   ☐ ½ cup chicken stock   ☐ Oil for
deep-frying   ☐ 1 tsp cornstarch, combined with a little water
☐ Salt and pepper

1. Steam the rice and allow to dry at room temperature.

2. Shell and devein the prawns.

3. In a frying pan, heat the oil, and briefly sauté first the ginger and
garlic and then the prawns. Remove and set aside. Sauté the red and
green peppers, onion and cucumber until cooked.

4. Add the soy sauce, orange juice, vinegar, sugar, chicken stock and
salt and pepper to taste.

5. Return the prawns to the pan and cook over a low heat for
approximately 10 minutes.

6. Meanwhile, heat the oil for deep-frying to 340°F. Form the glutinous
rice into balls and fry until golden. Drain them on paper towels and
place in a warm oven.

7. Thicken the prawns and sauce with the cornstarch, and serve poured
over the rice balls.

☐ TIME   Preparation takes about 20 minutes and cooking takes
about 15 minutes.

☐ CHECKPOINT   The steaming and drying of glutinous rice is a
lengthy process and should be done in advance.

☐

OPPOSITE

DEEP-FRIED
STICKY RICE
WITH PRAWNS

---- SERVES 4 ----

STEAMED SHRIMP

*Fresh shrimp, garnished with zucchini peel, steamed and served
with a fish flavored sauce.*

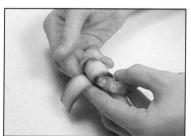

Step 3

☐ 1 tbsp fish sauce   ☐ 1 tbsp water   ☐ 1 tbsp wine vinegar
☐ 1 tbsp soy sauce   ☐ 2 tsps sugar   ☐ 10 fresh mint leaves, finely
chopped   ☐ 1 shallot, chopped   ☐ Salt and pepper   ☐ 12 fresh
shrimp, peeled and cleaned   ☐ 2 medium-sized zucchini, peeled and
the peel cut into long strips

1. Mix together the fish sauce, water, vinegar, soy sauce, sugar, mint, shallot and salt and pepper. Stir well and set aside for at least 1 hour.

2. Just before serving time, season the shrimp with plenty of salt and pepper.

3. Roll the strips of zucchini peel around the shrimp and cook them in a Chinese steamer for 5 minutes.

4. Serve the shrimp piping hot, accompanied with the sauce.

☐ TIME   Preparation takes about 20 minutes and cooking takes about 10 minutes for 2 batches.

☐ COOK'S TIP   If the strips of zucchini peel are not very pliable, blanch them in boiling water for 30 seconds, before wrapping round the shrimp.

☐ COOK'S TIP   The sauce can be prepared just before cooking the shrimp, but it is much tastier if prepared at least 1 hour in advance.

☐

OPPOSITE

STEAMED SHRIMP

—— SERVES 4 ——

SEAFOOD CHOW MEIN

*Chinese noodles cooked with mussels, cockles and vegetables and
served in a rich ginger and wine flavored sauce.*

Step 3

Step 4

☐ 8oz Chinese noodles   ☐ ½ green pepper, seeded
☐ ½ red pepper, seeded   ☐ 1 tbsp oil   ☐ ½ tsp chopped garlic
☐ ½ tsp chopped fresh ginger root   ☐ ½ scallion, chopped   ☐ 1 cup
uncooked mussels (shelled)   ☐ ⅓ cup uncooked cockles (shelled)
☐ 1 tbsp Chinese wine   ☐ 2 tbsps soy sauce   ☐ Salt and pepper

1. Cook the noodles in boiling, salted water. Rinse them under cold water and set aside to drain.

2. Cut the peppers into thin slices.

3. Heat the oil in a wok and stir-fry the garlic, ginger, peppers and scallion for 1 minute.

4. Stir in the mussels, cockles, Chinese wine, soy sauce and the cooked noodles.

5. Mix together well, using chopsticks. Season with salt and pepper and serve when cooked through completely.

☐ TIME   Preparation takes about 15 minutes and cooking takes approximately 15 minutes.

☐ VARIATION   Add other types of seafood to this dish.

☐ CHECKPOINT   In Step 5 heat the noodles through thoroughly, turning them in the sauce, to coat evenly.

☐

OPPOSITE

SEAFOOD CHOW
MEIN

---- SERVES 4 ----

CHICKEN WITH LEMON SAUCE

*Quick-fried chicken served with dried Chinese black mushrooms
in a lemon and ginger sauce.*

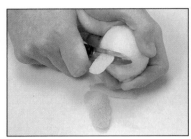

Step 1

Step 2

□ 1 lemon, washed   □ 2 tbsps dried Chinese black mushrooms,
soaked for 15 minutes in warm water   □ 2 tbsps oil   □ 1 chicken,
boned and the meat cut into thin slices   □ 1 tsp chopped fresh ginger
root   □ 1 tsp wine vinegar   □ 1 tbsp soy sauce   □ 1¼ cups chicken
stock   □ 1 tsp sugar   □ Salt and pepper

1. Peel the lemon with a potato peeler.

2. Cut the peel into thin julienne.

3. Blanch the julienne in boiling water and set aside to drain.

4. Squeeze and reserve the juice of the lemon.

5. Cook the reconstituted mushrooms in boiling, lightly salted water for
15 minutes and then rinse them in cold water. Drain the mushrooms
thoroughly, and slice them thinly.

6. Heat the oil in a wok and stir-fry the chicken, ginger and lemon peel
for 2 minutes.

7. Pour off any excess fat and deglaze the pan with the vinegar. Stir in
the lemon juice, soy sauce, stock, sugar and mushrooms.

8. Reduce the heat and cook for 20 minutes. Season with salt and
pepper to taste and serve hot.

□ TIME   Soaking the mushrooms takes 15 minutes, preparation
takes about 25 minutes and cooking takes approximately 30 minutes.

□ SERVING IDEA   Serve with steamed or boiled rice.

□ COOK'S TIP   The lemon peel must be blanched before using, or it
will give a bitter flavor to the dish.

□

OPPOSITE

**CHICKEN WITH
LEMON SAUCE**

SERVES 4

STUFFED CHICKEN LEGS

*For this appetizing dish, chicken legs are stuffed and rolled, then
steamed and served in a light ginger sauce.*

Step 2

Step 3

Step 3

□ 2 tbsps dried Chinese black mushrooms, soaked for 15 minutes in warm water   □ 4 chicken legs, boned   □ 1 egg, beaten
□ ½ tsp finely chopped fresh ginger root   □ 1¼ cups chicken stock
□ ½ tsp sugar   □ Salt and pepper   □ 1 tsp cornstarch, combined with a little water

---

1. Drain the mushrooms and cut them into thin slices.

2. Flatten out each piece of leg meat and brush a little beaten egg over the inside. Place the mushroom slices evenly over the 4 pieces of meat and sprinkle on half the ginger.

3. Roll up each piece of meat and secure with thin kitchen string. Steam the stuffed rolls for approximately 25 minutes, or until cooked.

4. Bring the stock to the boil and allow to reduce by half. Add the remaining ginger and the sugar and season with salt and pepper to taste.

5. Add the cornstarch to the sauce, stirring continuously until the desired consistency is reached.

6. Cut the string from the chicken rolls. Serve the chicken rolls sliced into rounds and topped with the sauce.

□ TIME   Soaking the mushrooms takes 15 minutes, preparation takes about 10 minutes and cooking takes approximately 30 minutes.

□ VARIATION   Enrich the sauce with a few reconstituted Chinese mushrooms. Cut them into thin julienne and add to the sauce in Step 4.

□ CHECKPOINT   The time required to cook the rolls will vary depending on their thickness; 25 minutes for thin rolls, slightly longer for thicker rolls.

□

OPPOSITE

STUFFED
CHICKEN LEGS

—— SERVES 4 ——

CHICKEN BREASTS
WITH SCALLION

*Stuffed chicken breasts, steamed and served
in a light soy-based sauce.*

□ 1 scallion, cut into rounds □ 1 carrot, cut into thin julienne
□ 1 tsp chopped garlic □ 4 chicken breasts □ Salt and pepper
□ ¾ cup chicken stock □ 1 tbsp soy sauce □ ½ tsp sugar
□ 1 tsp cornstarch, combined with a little water

Step 2

Step 3

Step 4

1. Mix together the scallion, carrot and half the garlic.

2. Slice the chicken breasts open lengthwise, without cutting through them completely.

3. Season the insides with salt and pepper and cover each breast with ¼ of the vegetable stuffing.

4. Pull the top half of the breast back into place. Season with salt and pepper. Steam for approximately 15 minutes until cooked through.

5. Bring the stock to the boil in a small saucepan. Stir in the soy sauce, sugar and the remaining garlic, simmer and allow to reduce for a few minutes.

6. Thicken the sauce by adding the dissolved cornstarch and stirring continuously until the desired consistency is reached.

7. Cut the stuffed chicken breasts into slices and serve them topped with sauce.

□ TIME   Preparation takes about 10 minutes and cooking takes approximately 25 minutes.

□ SERVING IDEA   Serve with plain boiled or steamed rice, garnished with 1 tbsp chopped fresh chives.

□ CHECKPOINT   The scallion and the carrot must be cut very thinly in order that they cook quickly during steaming.

□

OPPOSITE

CHICKEN
BREASTS WITH
SCALLION

—— SERVES 4 ——

CHICKEN WITH BAMBOO SHOOTS

Quick-fried chicken and bamboo shoots, served in a light ginger and oyster sauce.

Step 1

Step 1

□ 1 cup whole bamboo shoots or canned, sliced bamboo shoots
□ 1 tbsp sesame oil   □ 1 chicken, boned and the meat cut into thin slices   □ 1 tsp chopped garlic   □ ½ tsp chopped fresh ginger root
□ 1 tbsp Shaohsing wine   □ 1 tbsp oyster sauce   □ 1¼ cups chicken stock   □ Salt and pepper   □ 1 tsp cornstarch, combined with a little water

1. Cut the bamboo shoots in half lengthwise and then cut into thin, half-moonshaped slices.

2. Blanch the slices of bamboo shoot in boiling water, drain and rinse in cold water. Set aside to drain thoroughly.

3. Heat the sesame oil in a wok and stir-fry the chicken, garlic and ginger.

4. Pour off any excess fat. Deglaze the wok with the wine.

5. Stir in the oyster sauce and the stock.

6. Add the bamboo shoots, season with salt and pepper and cook for 2 minutes.

7. Thicken the sauce by stirring in the cornstarch and stirring continuously until the sauce reaches the desired consistency. Serve hot.

□ TIME   Preparation takes about 20 minutes and cooking takes approximately 10 minutes.

□ CHECKPOINT   Sesame oil gives a very strong flavor to this dish, so use half peanut oil and half sesame oil, if preferred.

□

OPPOSITE

CHICKEN WITH
BAMBOO SHOOTS

—— SERVES 4 ——

BRAISED CHICKEN WITH GINGER

Boned chicken, coated with ginger and cooked in a vegetable and ginger-flavored stock.

Step 5

Step 5

☐ 1 chicken, boned   ☐ ½ tsp chopped fresh ginger root   ☐ 1 carrot, cut into small cubes   ☐ 1 turnip, cut into small cubes   ☐ 1 zucchini, cut into small cubes   ☐ 1 onion, thinly sliced   ☐ 5 slices fresh ginger root   ☐ Salt and pepper

1. Separate the breast and the leg meat from the boned chicken. Keep each leg in one piece.

2. Place the remaining meat and the bones from the chicken in a saucepan, with just enough water to cover. Boil until the liquid has reduced to a quarter. Strain the stock through a fine sieve.

3. Sprinkle the chopped ginger on the inside of the 2 pieces of leg meat and season with salt and pepper. Roll up tightly and secure with kitchen string.

4. Add ½ cup water to the stock and bring to the boil in a saucepan.

5. Add the prepared vegetables, sliced ginger, rolled leg meat and the 2 breasts. Cook for approximately 35 minutes or until the chicken is cooked through.

6. Take out the rolled leg meat, cut off the string and cut the meat into rounds. Spread the slices on a warmed serving plate.

7. Take out the chicken breasts and slice them thinly. Arrange the slices on the warmed plate with the leg meat. Remove the vegetables using a slotted spoon, arrange them around the meat and then pour over a little of the stock.

8. Serve piping hot.

☐ TIME   Preparation takes about 20 minutes and cooking takes approximately 1 hour.

☐ VARIATION   If you do not want to use the chicken for the stock, use a stock cube dissolved in water.

☐ COOK'S TIP   If you are short of time, do not bone the legs, but simply cut slits in the meat and place the ginger in the slits.

☐

OPPOSITE

BRAISED CHICKEN WITH GINGER

―――― SERVES 4 ――――

CHICKEN WITH BEAN SPROUTS

*Marinated chicken, stir-fried with bean sprouts and served
with a sauce based on the marinade.*

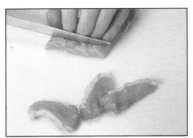

Step 1

Step 2

☐ 1 chicken, boned ☐ 1 tbsp Chinese wine ☐ 1 tsp cornstarch
☐ 1 cup bean sprouts ☐ 2 tbsps oil ☐ ½ scallion, finely sliced
☐ 1 tsp sugar ☐ 1¼ cups chicken stock ☐ Salt and pepper

1. Bone the chicken and cut the meat into thin slices or strips.

2. Place the chicken on a plate and pour over the Chinese wine.

3. Sprinkle over the cornstarch and stir together well. Leave to marinate for 30 minutes.

4. Blanch the bean sprouts in boiling, lightly salted water for 1 minute. Rinse under cold running water and set aside to drain.

5. Remove the chicken from the marinade with a spoon. Heat the oil in a wok and stir-fry the onions and the chicken.

6. Add the drained bean sprouts and the sugar. Stir in the marinade and the stock. Allow the chicken to cook through, which will take approximately 20 minutes. Check the seasoning, adding salt and pepper to taste. Serve immediately.

☐ TIME   Preparation takes about 20 minutes, marinating takes 30 minutes and cooking takes approximately 30 minutes.

☐ VARIATION   Use an ordinary onion if scallion is not available.

☐ CHECKPOINT   As soon as you add the marinade to the wok, the mixture will thicken, so have the stock ready to pour in immediately and stir continuously until all the ingredients have been fully incorporated.

☐

OPPOSITE

CHICKEN WITH
BEAN SPROUTS

--- SERVES 4 ---

CHICKEN IN HOT PEPPER SAUCE

Stir-fried chicken served with peppers in a hot pepper sauce.

Step 1

Step 1

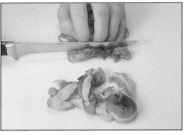

Step 1

☐ 2 tbsps oil ☐ 1 tsp chopped garlic ☐ 1 chicken ☐ 1 red pepper, seeded and cut into thin strips ☐ 1 green pepper, seeded and cut into thin strips ☐ 1 tsp wine vinegar ☐ 1 tbsp light soy sauce ☐ 1 tsp sugar ☐ 1¼ cups chicken stock ☐ 1 tbsp chili sauce ☐ Salt and pepper

1. First, bone the chicken. To bone the legs, cut down along the bone on all sides, drawing out the bone with an even movement. Cut all the chicken meat into thin strips. Heat the oil in a wok and stir-fry the garlic, chicken and the green and red peppers.

2. Pour off any excess oil and deglaze the wok with the vinegar. Stir in the soy sauce, sugar and stock.

3. Gradually stir in the chili sauce, tasting after each addition. Season with a little salt and pepper to taste.

4. Cook until the sauce has reduced slightly. Serve piping hot.

☐ TIME   Preparation takes about 10 minutes and cooking takes approximately 25 minutes.

☐ VARIATION   A fresh hot chili pepper could be used instead of the chili sauce. Seed it and chop very finely. Add sparingly to the wok and taste the sauce 1 minute after each addition: the flavor develops as the pepper is heated. Repeat the process to taste.

☐ SERVING IDEA   Serve with plain boiled or steamed rice.

☐

OPPOSITE

CHICKEN IN HOT
PEPPER SAUCE

---------------- SERVES 4 ----------------

DUCK WITH MANGOES

Oven-cooked duck breasts, served with sliced mango and coated in a mango sauce.

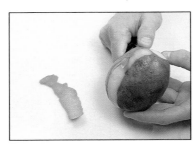

Step 1

Step 1

☐ 2 ripe mangoes ☐ 1¼ cups duck stock ☐ 2 duck breasts ☐ 1 tsp each finely chopped fresh ginger root and garlic ☐ Salt and pepper ☐ 2 tbsps oil ☐ 1 tsp vinegar ☐ 1 tbsp finely chopped fresh chives

1. Peel the mangoes. Using a sharp knife, cut the flesh through to the stone in several places all round each mango. Ease away the slices.

2. In a blender, blend the slices from half a mango with the stock until smooth.

3. Rub the duck breasts with the garlic and ginger and season with salt and pepper. Heat the oil in a frying pan and seal the duck breasts all over.

4. Remove the duck breasts from the frying pan and finish cooking in a preheated, hot oven, 425°F, for 15-20 minutes.

5. In a small saucepan, reduce the mango stock mixture with the vinegar, adding salt and pepper to taste.

6. Heat the remaining mango slices in a steamer for 1 minute.

7. Slice the duck breasts and serve them with the hot mango slices topped with the sauce. Sprinkle with the chives just before serving.

☐ TIME Preparation takes about 15 minutes and cooking takes approximately 30 minutes.

☐ CHECKPOINT Cut the mangoes into thick slices, as they tend to become rather fragile when heated.

☐ MICROWAVE TIP Place the slices of cold mango onto 4 plates and heat them individually for 1 minute.

☐

OPPOSITE

DUCK WITH
MANGOES

---- SERVES 4 ----

DUCKLING SALAD WITH SWEET AND SOUR SAUCE

A light, tasty salad to serve as an appetizer to a summer meal.

Step 5

□ 1 cooked duckling, cooled and boned   □ ½ cucumber
□ 2 carrots   □ 2 tbsps wine vinegar   □ 1 tsp mustard   □ 1 tsp sugar
□ 1 tbsp soy sauce   □ ½ tbsp hoisin sauce   □ 1 tsp sesame oil
□ 1 tbsp oil, preferably peanut   □ Salt and pepper

1. Cut the duckling meat into bite-sized chunks

2. Cut the cucumber into thin slices.

3. Cut the carrots into thin julienne.

4. In a small bowl, whip together the vinegar, mustard and sugar.

5. Add the soy sauce, followed by the hoisin sauce.

6. Lastly, whip in the oils and season with salt and pepper to taste.

7. Divide the duckling meat and the vegetables evenly between 4 small plates, pour a little of the sauce over each portion and serve.

□ TIME   Preparation takes about 20 minutes.

□ CHECKPOINT   Do not overcook the duckling, the meat for this salad should still be tender and juicy.

□ VARIATION   A variety of appropriate vegetables, such as bean sprouts, could be added. Duck breasts could be used instead of duckling.

□

OPPOSITE

DUCKLING
SALAD WITH
SWEET AND
SOUR SAUCE

———— SERVES 4 ————

DUCK WITH GINGER SAUCE

Ginger-stuffed rolls of duck meat, stir-fried and served in
a delicious, smooth ginger sauce.

Step 1

Step 1

☐ 4 duck legs ☐ 10 slices peeled fresh ginger root ☐ 2 tbsps oil
☐ 1 scallion, chopped ☐ 1 tsp chopped garlic ☐ 1 tbsp soy sauce
☐ 1¼ cups duck stock ☐ 1 tsp cornstarch, combined with a little water
☐ Salt and pepper

1. Chop off the ends of the duck legs and discard. Using a small sharp knife, slide the blade down the sides of the thigh bone and ease away all the meat. Cut the thigh meat into large slices. Cut the slices of ginger into fine julienne.

2. Place a little ginger on each slice of meat, roll up and secure with thin kitchen string.

3. Heat the oil in a wok and stir-fry the scallion with the garlic. Add the duck rolls, together with any leftover duck meat and fry for 2 minutes.

4. Pour off any excess fat.

5. Stir in the soy sauce, any leftover ginger and the stock. Allow to cook through completely.

6. Thicken the sauce with the cornstarch if desired. Check the seasoning, adding salt and pepper as necessary.

7. Cut off the string from each roll and serve hot, with the sauce.

☐ TIME Preparation takes about 25 minutes and cooking takes approximately 20 minutes.

☐ VARIATION If the ginger julienne are blanched before use, it gives a milder taste to the dish.

☐ SERVING IDEA If there is no time to assemble the rolls, simply stir-fry small pieces of duck with the ginger julienne and continue as before.

☐

OPPOSITE

DUCK WITH
GINGER SAUCE

LACQUERED "PEKING" DUCK

*Duck breasts marinated in honey and soy sauce for 24 hours
and baked in an ordinary oven.*

☐ ½ tsp soy sauce ☐ 1 tbsp honey ☐ 1 tsp five-spice powder
☐ 1 tsp wine vinegar ☐ 1 tsp chopped garlic ☐ 1 tsp cornstarch,
combined with a little water ☐ 2 duck breasts ☐ Salt and pepper

Step 1

Step 3

1. To make the marinade, mix together the soy sauce and the honey.

2. Sprinkle over the five-spice powder and stir in well.

3. Stir in the vinegar, garlic and cornstarch.

4. Season the breasts with a little salt and pepper and place in an ovenproof pan. Pour the marinade over to coat the duck breasts entirely. Leave to marinate for 24 hours.

5. Cook the breasts in a hot oven, 425°F, for approximately 20 minutes, basting frequently with the marinade.

6. To caramelize the tops, put under a hot broiler for several minutes until crisp. Watch carefully to prevent them burning.

☐ TIME   Marinating takes 24 hours, preparation takes about 5 minutes and cooking takes approximately 25 minutes.

☐ COOK'S TIP   Start cooking the duck breasts skin side up, and turn them over during cooking. Turn again to glaze the skin side under a hot broiler, before serving.

☐ SERVING IDEA   To serve more people, make twice as much marinade and use a whole duck. Score the skin for the marinade to penetrate and cook the duck in the oven for about 45 minutes to 1 hour.

☐

OPPOSITE

LACQUERED
"PEKING" DUCK

SERVES 4

DUCKLING IN FIVE-SPICE SAUCE

*Duckling slices cooked with water chestnuts, Chinese mushrooms
and bamboo shoots and served in a five-spice sauce.*

Step 1

Step 1

□ 12 canned water chestnuts   □ ½ cup bamboo shoots   □ 1 tbsp
sesame oil   □ 1 tsp chopped fresh ginger root   □ 1 duckling, boned
and the meat cut into thin slices   □ 4 dried Chinese mushrooms,
soaked in warm water for 15 minutes, drained and chopped
□ 1¼ cups duck stock   □ 1 tsp five-spice powder   □ Salt and pepper
□ 1 tsp cornstarch, combined with a little water

1. Rinse the water chestnuts and blanch in boiling, lightly salted water
for 10 minutes. Lift out and set them aside to drain.

2. Blanch the bamboo shoots in the same water, rinse and then drain.
Once well-drained, cut them into thin matchsticks.

3. Heat the sesame oil in a wok and stir-fry the ginger and the duckling
slices.

4. Remove the ginger and duckling with a slotted spoon and stir-fry the
bamboo shoots, chopped Chinese mushrooms and water chestnuts.

5. Pour off any excess fat and return the duckling and the ginger to the
wok with the previous ingredients. Add the duck stock and stir well.
Sprinkle over the fivespice powder and allow to cook for
approximately 15 minutes.

6. Check the seasoning, adding salt and pepper as necessary. Thicken
the sauce by stirring in the cornstarch, stirring continuously until the
desired consistency is reached. Serve hot.

□ TIME   Preparation takes about 25 minutes and cooking takes
approximately 30 minutes.

□ VARIATION   If you have no duck stock, use chicken stock instead.
Duck breasts may be used instead of duckling.

□ CHECKPOINT   The water chestnuts will remain very crunchy, but
they are not undercooked.

□

OPPOSITE

DUCKLING IN
FIVE-SPICE SAUCE

── SERVES 4 ──

DUCK WITH BAMBOO SHOOTS

*Stir-fried bamboo shoots, served with duck breasts and
a hoisin-based sauce.*

Step 3

Step 4

□ 1 cup bamboo shoots, cut into thin slices   □ ¼ cup sugar
□ ¾ cup water   □ 1 tsp chopped fresh ginger root   □ 1 tbsp hoisin
sauce   □ 2 duck breasts   □ 1 tbsp oil   □ Salt and pepper

1. Cook the bamboo shoots in boiling, lightly salted water for
approximately 15 minutes. Drain thoroughly and set aside.

2. Mix the sugar and water together in a small saucepan, stirring
thoroughly.

3. Add the ginger and the hoisin sauce. Place over a gentle heat and
cook until a light syrup is formed.

4. Brush this syrup liberally over the duck breasts.

5. Heat the oil in a frying pan and add the duck breasts, skin-side down
first. Sear on each side. Take out and finish cooking in a hot oven,
425°F, for approximately 15 minutes.

6. Shortly before the duck breasts are cooked, stir-fry the bamboo
shoots in the oil used to sear the duck breasts. Season with salt and
pepper and serve hot with the sliced duck breasts.

□   TIME   Preparation takes about 10 minutes and total cooking time
is approximately 50 minutes.

□   SERVING IDEA   Serve any leftover sauce in a small bowl to
accompany the duck.

□   CHECKPOINT   Don't forget to begin searing the meat in the
frying pan skin-side down and then finish with the other side.

□

OPPOSITE

DUCK WITH
BAMBOO SHOOTS

SERVES 4

DUCKLING WITH ONIONS

*Stir-fried onions and duckling, served in a rich sauce flavored with
Chinese wine, soy sauce and hoisin sauce.*

Step 1

Step 2

☐ 2 tbsps oil   ☐ 2 large onions, finely sliced   ☐ 1 duckling, boned
and the meat cut into slices   ☐ 2 tbsps Chinese wine   ☐ 1 tbsp soy
sauce   ☐ 1 tbsp hoisin sauce   ☐ 1¼ cups chicken stock
☐ Salt and pepper

---

1. Heat the oil in a wok and stir-fry the onion until lightly browned.
Ease the onions up the side of the wok out of the oil, to keep them
warm.

2. Add the duckling to the wok and stir-fry until lightly browned.

3. Pour in the Chinese wine. Push the onions back into the bottom of
the wok, with the duckling.

4. Stir in the soy sauce, hoisin sauce and the stock. Allow to cook until
slightly reduced.

5. Season with salt and pepper and serve immediately.

☐ TIME   Preparation takes about 15 minutes and cooking takes
approximately 15 minutes.

☐ VARIATION   If duckling is not available, use duck breasts.

☐

OPPOSITE

DUCKLING
WITH ONIONS

─── SERVES 4 ───

DUCKLING WITH CASHEW NUTS

*Sliced duckling, cooked with fresh cashew nuts and served
in a slightly sweet sauce.*

Step 1

Step 1

☐ 10 fresh cashew nuts   ☐ 2 tbsps oil   ☐ ½ tsp chopped garlic
☐ 1 duckling, boned and the meat cut into slices   ☐ 1 scallion,
chopped   ☐ 2 tbsps soy sauce   ☐ 1 cup chicken stock
☐ ½ tsp vinegar   ☐ 1 tsp sugar   ☐ Salt and pepper

1. Shell the cashew nuts, using either the blunt side of a chopping knife or a nutcracker. Remove the nuts from their shells and then slice into thin strips, using a very sharp knife.

2. Heat the oil in a wok and stir-fry the garlic and duckling until the meat is seared and browned.

3. Add the cashew nuts and the scallion and stir-fry for 1 minute. Pour off any excess fat.

4. Stir in the soy sauce, then the stock, vinegar and sugar. Season with salt and pepper.

5. Continue cooking until the duckling is tender and the sauce has reduced enough to coat the pieces of meat lightly.

☐   TIME   Preparation takes about 15 minutes and cooking takes approximately 20 minutes.

☐   VARIATION   Use different nuts, such as brazil nuts, almonds or hazelnuts. Duck breasts could be used instead of duckling.

NB Step-by-step pictures show preparation of Brazil nuts, which may be used as a substitute for cashew nuts in this dish.

☐

OPPOSITE

DUCKLING WITH
CASHEW NUTS

SERVES 4

DUCK WITH CORIANDER SAUCE

Duck stuffed with scallion, bamboo shoots and Chinese mushrooms, served in a coriander flavored sauce.

Step 2

Step 2

Step 3

Step 4

□ 1 duck, boned, leg and breast meat reserved   □ 1 scallion
□ ¼ cup bamboo shoots, blanched   □ 2 dried Chinese mushrooms, soaked for 15 minutes in warm water and drained   □ 10 coriander seeds   □ 1¼ cups duck stock   □ 1 tsp cornstarch, combined with a little water   □ Salt and pepper

1. Skin the duck breasts and reserve both meat and skin.

2. In a food processor process each of the following ingredients separately. One duck breast should be finely processed and then the scallion, the bamboo shoots and the Chinese mushrooms should all be lightly processed. Mix all the processed ingredients together in a small bowl.

3. Spread this stuffing mixture onto the boned leg meat and the remaining breast.

4. Roll the meat around the stuffing and wrap each one in plastic wrap. Twist the ends to seal well.

5. Steam the duck rolls in a steamer for 35 minutes.

6. Crush the coriander seeds and put into a small saucepan. Add the duck stock and cook over a gentle heat until reduced by a quarter. Thicken, if necessary, with the cornstarch, stirring continuously until the desired consistency is reached. Season to taste with salt and pepper.

7. Heat the oil in a frying pan and fry the reserved duck skin until crisp. Leave to cool and then cut into small pieces.

8. Remove the plastic wrap from the duck. Serve the rolls sliced into rounds, with some of the crispy skin pieces and the sauce.

□ TIME   Preparation takes about 30 minutes and cooking takes approximately 50 minutes.

□ PREPARATION   Either cook the remaining duck meat at the same time as you steam the rolls or keep it for another dish.

□ VARIATION   If available, add some chopped fresh coriander to the sauce.

□

OPPOSITE

DUCK WITH
CORIANDER
SAUCE

SERVES 4

CARAMELIZED SPARERIBS

*These sweet, caramelized spareribs are always a success. Tell guests
to use their fingers; knives or chopsticks are out of the question.*

Step 2

Step 3

□ 1 carrot   □ 1 leek   □ 1 bay leaf   □ 2lbs pork spareribs, separated
□ 1 tbsp honey   □ 1 tbsp white wine vinegar   □ 1 tsp chopped garlic
□ 2 tbsps soy sauce   □ ¼ cup chicken stock   □ Salt and pepper

1. In a large saucepan combine 4 cups water with the carrot, bay leaf
and leek. Bring to the boil and add the spareribs. Blanch the meat for
10 minutes, remove from the stock and drain well.

2. Lay the ribs in an ovenproof pan. Combine the honey, vinegar and
garlic, and spread the mixture on the ribs.

3. Add the soy sauce and the stock to the dish. Season well with salt
and pepper.

4. Put into a very hot oven, 475°F, and cook until the ribs are
caramelized and have turned a rich, dark brown color.

□ TIME   Preparation takes about 5 minutes and cooking takes
approximately 55 minutes, from start to finish.

□ SERVING IDEA   Serve on a bed of finely shredded lettuce leaves,
lightly seasoned with salt and pepper.

□

OPPOSITE

CARAMELIZED
SPARERIBS

RICE-COATED MEATBALLS

*These highly seasoned meatballs, coated in pre-soaked rice, could
also be made using any type of meat.*

Step 1

Step 2

☐ ¾ cup long grain rice, pre-soaked in warm water for 2 hours
☐ 1½lbs boned pork shoulder, ground   ☐ 1-inch piece fresh ginger
root, peeled and chopped   ☐ ½ tsp shallots, finely chopped
☐ ½ tsp finely chopped fresh parsley   ☐ ½ tsp finely chopped fresh
chives   ☐ ½ tsp soy sauce   ☐ ½ egg, beaten   ☐ Tip of a knife of
chili sauce   ☐ Salt and pepper

1. Mix together the meat, ginger, shallots, parsley, chives, soy sauce, egg
and chili sauce. Beat well to combine all the ingredients.

2. Season with salt and pepper and then form into small meatballs.

3. Drain the rice very carefully, shaking well to remove all the water.
Spread the rice on your work surface.

4. Roll the meatballs in the rice to coat them evenly.

5. Steam the meatballs for approximately 15 minutes. The exact
cooking time will depend on the thickness of your meatballs, but small
ones take 15 minutes.

☐ TIME   Pre-soaking the rice takes 2 hours, preparation takes about
30 minutes and cooking takes approximately 15-20 minutes if you can
steam all the meatballs in one batch, longer if you need to do two
batches.

☐ COOK'S TIP   Rinse your hands in cold water before shaping the
meatballs, otherwise they tend to stick and break up.

☐ VARIATION   Any type of meat can be used for these meatballs, so
try beef, veal or even chicken.

☐

OPPOSITE

RICE-COATED
MEATBALLS

SERVES 4

PORK IN SWEET AND SOUR SAUCE

Pork with matchstick vegetables in a marvellous sweet and sour sauce.

Step 5

Step 5

□ 1 onion   □ ¼ cucumber   □ ½ red pepper, seeded   □ ½ green pepper, seeded   □ 1 slice pineapple, fresh or canned   □ 4 tbsps pineapple juice   □ 3 tbsps wine vinegar   □ 1 tsp chili sauce   □ 1 tbsp sugar   □ ½ tomato, peeled, seeded and crushed   □ 1¼ cups chicken stock   □ 2 tbsps oil   □ 1 tsp cornstarch, mixed with 1 tsp water   □ 1lb pork, cut into thin strips   □ Salt and pepper   □ 1 clove garlic, chopped

1. Cut the onion, cucumber, red and green pepper and pineapple into thin matchsticks.

2. In a small bowl, mix together the pineapple juice, vinegar, chili sauce, sugar, crushed tomato and chicken stock.

3. Heat the oil in a wok, stir-fry the pork and the garlic. Once the meat is golden brown, remove with a slotted spoon and set aside.

4. Add all the vegetables and the pineapple to the wok and stir-fry for 2 minutes.

5. Return the pork to the wok with the vegetables and pineapple and pour over the contents of the bowl. Cook for 3-4 minutes, stirring, and shaking the wok from time to time.

6. Thicken the sauce by adding the cornstarch gradually, stirring continously until the desired consistency is reached. Season to taste with salt and pepper.

7. Serve piping hot.

□ TIME   Preparation takes about 25 minutes and cooking takes approximately 40 minutes.

□ VARIATION   Replace the pineapple juice with orange juice.

□ CHECKPOINT   The vegetables must be stir-fried quickly so that they remain slightly crisp.

□

OPPOSITE

PORK IN SWEET
AND SOUR
SAUCE

---SERVES 4---

PORK SLICES WITH
CRUNCHY VEGETABLES

*This dish has a cold sauce to accompany lightly steamed
vegetables and thinly sliced pork.*

Step 4

Step 4

□ 1 tbsp light soy sauce □ 1 tbsp Chinese wine □ 1 tsp sugar
□ 1-inch piece of fresh ginger root, peeled and finely chopped
□ 1lb lean pork □ Salt and pepper □ 1 carrot □ 1 stick celery
□ ½ fennel bulb

1. For the sauce, mix together the soy sauce, Chinese wine, sugar and ginger in a small bowl. Allow to stand for 30 minutes for the flavors to develop before serving.

2. Cut the pork into very thin slices and season with salt and pepper.

3. Cut the carrot, celery and fennel into thin julienne. Place them in a steaming basket and steam for 3 minutes.

4. Remove the basket from the steamer and lay the slices of pork over the vegetables. Return the basket to the steamer and cook for another 5 minutes.

5. Serve the steamed pork and vegetables accompanied with the cold sauce.

□ TIME   The sauce must stand for 30 minutes, preparation takes about 15 minutes and cooking takes approximately 8-10 minutes.

□ VARIATION   You can use any vegetables for this recipe.

□ CHECKPOINT   Carrots take longer to cook than celery and should therefore be cut into thinner strips to ensure even cooking.

□

OPPOSITE

PORK SLICES
WITH CRUNCHY
VEGETABLES

―――― SERVES 4 ――――

STIR-FRIED PORK
AND VEGETABLES

*A quick and easy stir-fry of pork, bean sprouts and carrot, served
in a spicy, slightly sweet sauce.*

Step 4

Step 5

☐ 1 carrot, cut into thin matchsticks   ☐ 1 cup bean sprouts
☐ 2 tbsps oil   ☐ Slice of fresh ginger root   ☐ 1 scallion, chopped
☐ ½ tsp chopped garlic   ☐ 1lb pork, cut into thin slices   ☐ 2 tsps sake
☐ 1¼ cups chicken stock   ☐ Salt and pepper   ☐ ½ tsp brown sugar
☐ 1 tsp cornstarch, combined with a little water

1. In a small saucepan, bring to the boil a little salted water. Blanch the julienned carrot in this water for 1 minute. Drain well, reserving the water.

2. Wash the bean sprouts in lots of running water and blanch for 1 minute in the water used for the carrot. Rinse well and drain.

3. Heat the oil in a wok. Stir-fry the ginger, scallion and the garlic until slightly colored.

4. Add the meat, stir in well and cook for 1 minute.

5. Add the well-drained vegetables, wine and stock. Season with salt and pepper, stir together well and cook for 2 minutes.

6. Using a slotted spoon, take out the meat and the vegetables, and keep warm.

7. Add the sugar to the contents of the wok and thicken the sauce with the cornstarch, adding it gradually and stirring continuously until the desired consistency is reached.

8. Remove the ginger, return the meat and vegetables to the wok and serve hot.

☐ TIME   Preparation takes about 25 minutes and cooking takes approximately 10 minutes.

☐ SERVING IDEA   Sprinkle a few drops of sesame oil over the finished dish.

☐ COOK'S TIP   Stir-fry the scallion and the ginger before the chopped garlic, as the garlic tends to stick and brown before the scallion is cooked.

☐

OPPOSITE

STIR-FRIED PORK
AND VEGETABLES

---- SERVES 4 ----

PORK WITH GREEN PEPPERS

A quickly-prepared stir-fried pork dish with green peppers and a hoisin-based sauce.

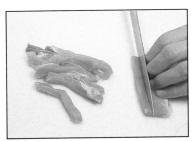
Step 1

☐ 1lb pork fillet ☐ 2 tbsps oil ☐ ½ tsp chopped garlic ☐ 2 green peppers, seeded and cut into thin matchsticks ☐ 1 tsp wine vinegar ☐ 2 tbsps chicken stock ☐ 1 tbsp hoisin sauce ☐ Salt and pepper ☐ 1 tsp cornstarch, combined with a little water

1. Slice the pork thinly, then cut into narrow strips. Heat the oil in a wok. Add the garlic, green pepper and the meat. Stir together well. Cook for 1 minute, shaking the wok occasionally.

2. Stir in the vinegar, stock and hoisin sauce. Season to taste with salt and pepper. Cook for 3 minutes.

3. Stir in the cornstarch and cook, stirring continuously, until the desired consistency is reached.

☐ TIME   Preparation takes about 10 minutes and cooking takes 5 minutes.

☐ VARIATION   Replace the green pepper with a red one.

☐ CHECKPOINT   It is not necessary to add sugar to this sauce, as the hoisin sauce is sweet enough.

☐

OPPOSITE

PORK WITH
GREEN PEPPERS

PORK SPARERIBS WITH CHINESE MUSHROOMS

Spareribs served with Chinese mushrooms in a slightly hot and spicy sauce.

Step 1

Step 1

Step 1

□ 2lbs pork spareribs   □ 1 carrot, finely sliced   □ 1 leek, finely chopped   □ 1 bay leaf   □ 6oz dried Chinese mushrooms, soaked for 15 minutes in warm water and drained   □ 1 tbsp oil   □ 1 tsp chopped garlic   □ ½ tsp chili sauce   □ 1 tbsp soy sauce   □ 1 tbsp hoisin sauce   □ 1 tsp wine vinegar   □ 1¼ cups chicken stock   □ Salt and pepper

1. Cut the spareribs down the bone to separate them. Now cut them into smaller pieces, so that they are easier to handle. In a medium-sized, flameproof casserole bring to the boil plenty of water to which you have added the carrot, leek and bay leaf. Blanch the spareribs for 1 minute in the boiling water. Drain well.

2. Cook the mushrooms in the boiling water for 10 minutes. Drain well.

3. Heat the oil in a wok, add the garlic, chili sauce and the mushrooms. Fry slowly until lightly colored.

4. Stir in the soy sauce, hoisin sauce, vinegar and stock.

5. Add the spareribs, stirring all the ingredients together well. Season with salt and pepper to taste and cook, covered, for 10 minutes.

6. Remove the lid and allow the sauce to reduce slightly. Serve piping hot.

□ TIME   Preparation takes about 15 minutes, soaking the mushrooms about 15 minutes and cooking takes approximately 20 minutes.

□ VARIATION   If you cannot buy hoisin sauce, replace it with 1 tsp sugar.

□ CHECKPOINT   You should not blanch the spareribs for longer than 1 minute.

□

OPPOSITE

PORK SPARERIBS WITH CHINESE MUSHROOMS

—— SERVES 4 ——

CARAMELIZED PORK

Paper thin slices of pork fillet cooked and served in a slightly sweet caramel sauce.

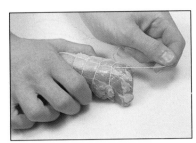

Step 3

Step 4

☐ 2 tbsps dark soy sauce   ☐ 1 tbsp Shaohsing wine   ☐ 1 tbsp hoisin sauce   ☐ 1 tsp honey   ☐ Few drops chili sauce   ☐ ½ tbsp oil   ☐ 1lb pork fillet   ☐ Salt and pepper

1. In a small bowl, mix together the soy sauce, Shaohsing wine, hoisin sauce, honey, chili sauce and the oil. Stir together well.

2. Cut off any excess fat from the pork fillet and remove any gristle and nerves.

3. Roll the fillet up and secure with thin kitchen string. Place the fillet in an ovenproof pan.

4. Pour over the prepared sauce and cook in a moderate oven, 350°F. Baste the roast with the sauce during cooking, so that it builds up in caramelized layers around the meat. The pork should be roasted until cooked through completely, which should take approximately 30 minutes.

5. Remove the roast from the oven and place the meat on a cutting board. Pour any remaining sauce into a sauce boat.

6. Cut the meat into paper thin slices and arrange on a warmed serving plate. Serve immediately with the remaining sauce.

☐ TIME   Preparation takes about 15 minutes and cooking takes approximately 30 minutes.

☐ SERVING IDEA   This dish can also be served cold with a mixed green side salad.

☐ CHECKPOINT   Should the bottom of the ovenproof pan start to burn during cooking, add a little water or stock.

☐

OPPOSITE

CARAMELIZED
PORK

—— SERVES 4 ——

PORK WITH BAMBOO SHOOTS

Stir-fried pork, served with bamboo shoots and zucchini.

Step 5

Step 5

☐ 1lb lean pork   ☐ 1 cup bamboo shoots   ☐ 1 zucchini
☐ 2 tbsps oil   ☐ 1 scallion, chopped   ☐ ½ cup chicken stock
☐ 1 tbsp soy sauce   ☐ 1 tsp cornstarch, combined with a little water
☐ Salt and pepper

1. Cut the pork into very thin slices and season with salt and pepper.

2. Cut the bamboo shoots into small squares and blanch in boiling, lightly salted water for 2 minutes. Drain well.

3. Using a sharp knife, peel the zucchini thickly lengthwise. Discard the remaining flesh and seeds. Slice the peel thinly.

4. Heat the oil in a wok, add the scallion and the meat. Stir-fry for 1 minute.

5. Pour off any excess fat and stir in the stock. Add the bamboo shoots and the zucchini. Cook gently for 7 minutes.

6. Stir in the soy sauce and add the cornstarch gradually, stirring continuously until the sauce has thickened. Add salt and pepper to taste. Serve hot.

☐ TIME   Preparation takes about 10 minutes and cooking takes approximately 15 minutes.

☐ COOK'S TIP   It is very important to blanch the bamboo shoots first to remove bitterness.

☐ ECONOMY   The inner part of the zucchini could be saved and used for another recipe, such as a purée.

☐

OPPOSITE

**PORK WITH
BAMBOO SHOOTS**

——— SERVES 4 ———

PORK WITH CHINESE VEGETABLES

*Marinated pork, stir-fried with mushrooms and bamboo shoots
and served in a ginger and garlic flavored sauce.*

Step 2

Step 2

Step 2

□ 1lb pork fillet   □ ½ tsp chopped garlic   □ ½ tsp chopped fresh
ginger root   □ ½ tsp cornstarch   □ Few drops chili sauce
□ 1 tbsp wine vinegar   □ 1 tbsp soy sauce   □ 1 cup bamboo shoots
□ 2oz dried Chinese black mushrooms, soaked for 15 minutes in
warm water   □ 2 tbsps oil   □ 1¼ cups chicken stock

1. Cut the pork into small cubes.

2. Place the garlic and ginger on top of the cubed meat. Sprinkle over the cornstarch. Add a few drops of chili sauce, but not too much as it is very hot, then the vinegar. Finally sprinkle over the soy sauce. The meat should now be left to marinate for 20 minutes at room temperature.

3. Cut the bamboo shoots into thin strips, blanch them in boiling, lightly salted water, rinse in cold water and set aside to drain.

4. Rinse the mushrooms and set aside to drain.

5. Remove the meat from the marinade with a slotted spoon. Reserve the marinade.

6. Heat the oil in a wok and sauté the meat. Pour off the excess fat and pour in the stock.

7. Stir in first the mushrooms and the bamboo shoots and then the marinade and cook together until thickened. Serve hot.

□ TIME   Marinating takes about 20 minutes, preparation takes about 10 minutes and cooking takes approximately 10 minutes.

□ COOK'S TIP   Since the marinade contains cornstarch, the sauce will thicken when cooked. Stir continuously to prevent lumps forming.

□

OPPOSITE

PORK WITH
CHINESE
VEGETABLES

PORK WITH SCRAMBLED EGGS

*Oyster flavored scrambled eggs with stir-fried pork
and Chinese mushrooms.*

Step 1

Step 4

Step 4

☐ 8 eggs ☐ ½ onion, chopped ☐ 1 tbsp oyster sauce ☐ Salt and pepper ☐ 1lb lean pork ☐ 2 tbsps oil ☐ ½ tsp chopped garlic ☐ ½ cup dried black Chinese mushrooms, soaked for 15 minutes in warm water ☐ 1 tsp sugar ☐ ½ tsp soy sauce ☐ 1 cup chicken stock ☐ 1 tsp cornstarch, combined with a little water

1. Beat the eggs together with the onion, oyster sauce and a little pepper. Set aside.

2. Cut the meat into very thin slices.

3. Rinse and drain the mushrooms.

4. Cook the eggs over a very gentle heat in a frying pan, stirring constantly with a wooden spoon or a spatula. This should take approximately 10 minutes.

5. Heat the oil in a wok and sauté the garlic and the pork. Pour off any excess fat and add the mushrooms, sugar, soy sauce and the stock. Cook until the meat is cooked through. Thicken with the cornstarch, adding it gradually and stirring continuously until the sauce thickens.

6. Place a bed of scrambled eggs on a warm plate and arrange the meat mixture over the eggs.

☐ TIME Preparation takes about 10 minutes, soaking the mushrooms takes 15 minutes and cooking takes approximately 30 minutes.

☐ VARIATION Add 1 tbsp of chopped fresh chives to the egg mixture before cooking, and sprinkle a little more over the finished dish. Any other herb could also be used.

☐ COOK'S TIP The cooking time for the scrambled eggs will depend on whether you prefer them cooked soft or dry.

☐

OPPOSITE

**PORK WITH
SCRAMBLED
EGGS**

————— SERVES 4 —————

PORK FRITTERS

Stir-fried pork, dipped in a light batter and deep-fried.

Step 2

Step 2

☐ 14oz pork tenderloin   ☐ 2 tbsps oil   ☐ 1½ cups all-purpose flour   ☐ 1½ tsps baking powder   ☐ 1 tsp grated lemon zest, blanched in boiling water   ☐ 1 egg, beaten   ☐ ½ cup milk   ☐ Oil for deep-frying   ☐ Salt and pepper

1. Cut the meat into thin slices or small cubes. Heat the oil in a wok and stir-fry the meat until almost cooked, which should take approximately 2 minutes. Drain and set aside.

2. Place the flour in a mixing bowl, add the baking powder and the lemon zest. Beat in the egg and the milk to form a smooth batter.

3. Heat the oil for deep-frying to 350°F.

4. Dip the slices or cubes of meat into the batter and lower into the preheated oil.

5. Fry until puffy and golden, then drain on paper towels. Serve hot, seasoned with salt and pepper.

☐ TIME   Preparation takes about 15 minutes and cooking, depending on how many batches you have to fry, takes approximately 35 minutes.

☐ SERVING IDEA   If you can obtain them, serve with zucchini flowers, also dipped into the batter and deep-fried.

☐ CHECKPOINT   Do not heat the oil above 350°F, or the batter will be done before the pork is cooked through.

☐

OPPOSITE

PORK FRITTERS

———— SERVES 4 ————

STUFFED CHINESE CABBAGE

These rolls are stuffed with a highly-flavored meat and vegetable mixture and served in a fragrant sauce.

Step 4

Step 4

Step 4

□ 8oz lean pork   □ 8oz boneless chicken   □ ½ cup Chinese cabbage   □ 1 tbsp oil   □ ½ tsp chopped garlic   □ ½ cup bean sprouts, blanched   □ 2 tbsps canned corn   □ 2 tbsps soy sauce   □ Salt and pepper   □ 1½ cups duck stock   □ 1 tsp cornstarch, combined with a little water

1. Chop the pork and the chicken finely.

2. Reserve 8 Chinese cabbage leaves. Shred the remaining leaves finely. Blanch the reserved leaves in boiling water, until soft, then refresh them in cold water and dry on a kitchen towel.

3. Heat the oil and stir-fry the meat, garlic, shredded Chinese cabbage, bean sprouts, corn, 1 tbsp of the soy sauce, salt and pepper for several minutes.

4. Spread out the blanched leaves and place a small amount of stuffing on each one. Roll up the leaf around the stuffing, beginning at the base and folding in the sides halfway up.

5. Heat together the stock and the remaining soy sauce. Put the stuffed rolls into the stock and cook for 5 minutes, turning occasionally.

6. Remove the rolls and place them on a heated serving plate.

7. Thicken the sauce by adding the cornstarch. Heat, stirring continuously, until the sauce thickens. Adjust the seasoning as necessary.

8. To serve, surround the rolls with the sauce, flavored with a few drops of soy sauce.

□ TIME   Preparation takes about 30 minutes and cooking takes approximately 15 minutes.

□ SERVING IDEA   Wrap a thin strip of blanched leek around each roll, sealing the leek to it with a little beaten egg.

□ CHECKPOINT   If the cabbage leaves are small, you will need to set aside 2 leaves per roll, making a total of 16 leaves, and overlap them around the stuffing.

□

OPPOSITE

STUFFED
CHINESE
CABBAGE

─── SERVES 4 ───

MEATBALLS WITH BAMBOO SHOOTS

Stir-fried meatballs with herbs and vegetables, served in a richly flavored sauce.

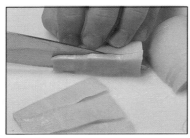

Step 3

Step 3

☐ 8oz lean pork 8oz boneless chicken ☐ 1 clove garlic, chopped ☐ 1 tbsp chopped chives ☐ 1 egg ☐ Salt and pepper ☐ 1¾ cups bamboo shoots ☐ 2 tbsps oil ☐ 1 scallion, chopped ☐ ½ tsp chopped fresh ginger root ☐ ¾ cup chicken stock ☐ 1 tsp cornstarch, combined with a little water

1. Mince the chicken and pork in a food processor with half the garlic and chives.

2. Place the meat in a bowl and add the egg. Beat well with a fork. Season with salt and pepper.

3. Cut the bamboo shoots into thin, even slices and blanch in boiling, salted water. Rinse under cold water and drain.

4. Heat 1 tbsp of the oil in a frying pan. Mold the meat in your hands to form small, flat rounds and fry on both sides until almost cooked.

5. Heat the remaining oil in a wok and stir-fry the scallion, remaining garlic and chives, the ginger and bamboo shoots for 2 minutes.

6. Stir in the chicken stock and allow to reduce. Season again with salt and pepper. Add the diluted cornstarch, stirring continuously until the sauce thickens.

7. Cut the meat rounds into even-sized strips and finish cooking in a Chinese steamer.

8. Serve the meat with the bamboo shoots and sauce.

☐ TIME   Preparation takes about 25 minutes and cooking takes approximately 40 minutes.

☐ VARIATION   Use any meat for this recipe.

☐ CHECKPOINT   The meat rounds are rather fragile; turn them over carefully so as not to break them. You may use a small plate as a support when turning them over.

☐

OPPOSITE

MEATBALLS WITH BAMBOO SHOOTS

BEEF WITH ONIONS

*Marinated beef, sautéed with onions, garlic and ginger
and served in a smooth sauce.*

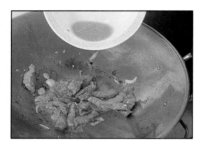

Step 5

Step 6

□ 1lb fillet steak

MARINADE

□ 1 tbsp oil   □ 1 tsp sesame oil   □ 1 tbsp Chinese wine   □ 1 tbsp oil
□ 1 piece fresh ginger root, peeled and roughly chopped   □ 3 onions,
finely sliced   □ 1 garlic clove, chopped   □ 1¼ cups beef stock
□ 1 pinch of sugar   □ 2 tbsps dark soy sauce   □ 1 tsp cornstarch,
combined with a little water   □ Salt and pepper

1. Cut the fillet into very thin slices.

2. Mix together the marinade ingredients and stir in the meat. Leave to marinate for 30 minutes.

3. Heat 1 tbsp oil in a wok and sauté the ginger, onions and garlic until lightly browned.

4. Lift the meat out of the marinade with a slotted spoon and discard the marinade. Add the meat to the wok and sauté with the vegetables.

5. Pour over the stock, sugar and soy sauce. Cook for 4 minutes.

6. Thicken the sauce with the cornstarch, stirring continuously until the desired consistency is reached. Season with salt and pepper and serve immediately.

□ TIME   Preparation takes about 15 minutes and cooking takes approximately 20 minutes.

□ SERVING IDEA   Serve this dish on a bed of boiled or steamed white rice.

□ CHECKPOINT   If you use a wok, watch the cooking process carefully, as the ingredients cook very quickly.

□

OPPOSITE

BEEF WITH
ONIONS

—— SERVES 4 ——

STIR-FRIED BEEF
WITH PINEAPPLE

*Sliced fillet steak cooked with pineapple and served
in a sweet and sour sauce.*

Step 2

Step 2

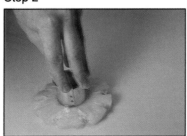

Step 3

☐ 1lb fillet steak ☐ ½ fresh pineapple ☐ 1 tbsp oil ☐ 1 scallion, chopped ☐ ½ tsp chopped fresh ginger root ☐ 1 tsp vinegar ☐ 1 tsp sugar ☐ 2 tsps light soy sauce ☐ 1¼ cups chicken stock ☐ ½ cup pineapple juice ☐ ½ tomato, seeded and chopped ☐ 1 tsp cornstarch, combined with a little water ☐ Salt and pepper

1. Cut the fillet steak into thin strips and season with salt and pepper.

2. Peel the pineapple and cut out all the brown 'eyes' from the flesh.

3. Cut into round slices, removing any tough parts parts and the core.

4. Cut the remaining flesh into small, even pieces.

5. Heat the oil in the wok. Add the onion, ginger and the meat and stir-fry until lightly colored.

6. Pour off any excess fat.

7. Stir in the vinegar, sugar, soy sauce, chicken stock and pineapple juice. Add the tomato and the pineapple pieces. Reduce the heat and cook for a few minutes.

8. Add the cornstarch gradually, stirring continuously until the desired consistency is reached.

☐ TIME Preparation takes about 15 minutes and cooking takes approximately 30 minutes.

☐ VARIATION Fresh pineapple juice could be used. Blend the remaining ½ pineapple and then pass it through a sieve. Make up to ½ cup with water if necessary.

☐ CHECKPOINT Cornstarch can be used to thicken many sauces, but always stir it in gradually, so that the sauce does not thicken too much.

☐

OPPOSITE

**STIR-FRIED BEEF
WITH PINEAPPLE**

SERVES 4

BEEF IN OYSTER SAUCE

Marinated beef, cooked and served in a ginger and oyster sauce.

Step 4

Step 5

☐ 1 tbsp sake   ☐ ½ tsp bicarbonate of soda   ☐ ½ tsp sugar
☐ 1lb fillet steak, cut into thin slices   ☐ 2 tbsps oil   ☐ 1 scallion,
chopped   ☐ ½ tsp chopped garlic   ☐ ½ tsp chopped fresh ginger
root   ☐ 1 tbsp green peppercorns   ☐ 2 tbsps oyster sauce
☐ 1¼ cups beef stock   ☐ 1 tsp cornstarch, combined with a little water
☐ Salt and pepper

1. Mix together the sake, bicarbonate of soda and the sugar. Place the sliced meat in the marinade and marinate at room temperature for 1 hour.

2. When the meat is ready to cook, heat the oil in a wok and briefly stir-fry the scallion, garlic, ginger and peppercorns.

3. Drain the meat, reserving the marinade.

4. Add the drained meat to the wok, stir well and cook for 1 minute. Pour off any excess oil.

5. Pour over the marinade, stir in the oyster sauce and the beef stock. Season well with salt and pepper.

6. Allow the sauce to reduce slightly. If it is still too thin, add a little of the cornstarch, stirring continously until the desired consistency is reached.

☐ TIME   Preparation takes about 20 minutes and cooking takes approximately 15 minutes.

☐ VARIATION   If green peppercorns are not available, use the mixed variety, but reduce the quantity by half.

☐ CHECKPOINT   This dish should be cooked rapidly, so that the meat does not dry out.

☐

OPPOSITE

BEEF IN OYSTER
SAUCE

SERVES 4

BEEF WITH BROCCOLI

A slightly hot sauce accompanies this dish of beef and broccoli.

Step 5

Step 5

Step 7

□ 1½lbs rib of beef □ ½lb broccoli □ 1 tbsp oil □ 1-inch piece fresh ginger root, peeled and finely chopped □ 1 tbsp sake □ 2 tsps chili sauce □ 1½ cups beef stock □ 2 tbsps dark soy sauce □ Salt and pepper □ 1 tsp cornstarch, combined with a little water

1. Cut the beef into small cubes. Do not remove any fat from the meat.

2. Cut off the hard stem from the broccoli and separate the flowerets. The stems may be reserved for another dish, such as a broccoli purée.

3. Bring a large quantity of salted water to the boil. Add the broccoli flowerets and cook until tender but still slightly crisp. Rinse immediately under cold water to stop the cooking process and then leave to drain.

4. Heat the oil in a wok and stir-fry the ginger and the meat.

5. Pour off any excess fat and deglaze the wok with the sake. Stir in the chili sauce, beef stock and the soy sauce. Cook over a gentle heat for 10 minutes.

6. Remove the meat with a slotted spoon and keep warm. Season the sauce with salt and pepper to taste.

7. Add the well-drained broccoli to the wok, allowing it to heat through completely. Remove with a slotted spoon and keep warm with the meat.

8. Add the cornstarch to the sauce in the wok, stirring continuously until the desired consistency is reached.

9. Serve the meat and broccoli topped with the sauce.

□ TIME Preparation takes about 20 minutes and cooking takes approximately 25 minutes.

□ VARIATION Replace the broccoli with cauliflower flowerets.

□ CHECKPOINT If you think there will not be enough sauce, add a little more beef stock before you thicken it with the cornstarch.

□

OPPOSITE

BEEF WITH
BROCCOLI

SERVES 4

BEEF WITH CHINESE MUSHROOMS

*Unlike most Chinese meat dishes, this one does not have a sauce.
The beef is first marinated and then simply dry-cooked
with the mushrooms.*

Step 1

Step 1

Step 1

☐ 1 tsp cornstarch   ☐ 1 tbsp light soy sauce   ☐ 1 egg white
☐ 1 tsp sugar   ☐ 1lb rump steak, thinly sliced   ☐ 6 dried Chinese
black mushrooms, soaked for 1 hour in warm water   ☐ 2 tbsps light
soy sauce   ☐ ½ tsp chopped garlic   ☐ Salt and pepper   ☐ 2 tbsps
Chinese wine

1. To make this unusual marinade, begin by placing the cornstarch in a small bowl. Stir in the soy sauce. Now beat in the egg white and the sugar, beating thoroughly to combine all the ingredients. Add the slices of beef and leave to marinate for 1 hour.

2. Drain the mushrooms, which should be very soft. Cut them into thin strips.

3. Transfer the beef from the marinade to a small plate, without draining.

4. Heat the oil in a wok, stir-fry the garlic, beef and the mushrooms until colored. Season with salt and pepper.

5. Stir in the wine and serve as soon as it has evaporated.

☐ TIME   Pre-soak the mushrooms for 1 hour. Marinating the beef takes 1 hour, preparation about 20 minutes and cooking takes approximately 10 minutes.

☐ SERVING IDEA   Serve with plain steamed rice or stir-fried rice and vegetables.

☐

OPPOSITE

BEEF WITH
CHINESE
MUSHROOMS

—— SERVES 4 ——

BEEF WITH GINGER SAUCE

*Quick-fried beef with fresh ginger root, served in
a soy and tomato sauce.*

Step 2

Step 3

☐ 1lb beef fillet   ☐ 2 tbsps oil   ☐ 2 tbsps fresh ginger root, peeled
and cut into small matchsticks   ☐ 2 tomatoes, peeled, seeded and
finely chopped   ☐ 1 tsp sugar   ☐ 1 tbsp red wine vinegar
☐ 2 tbsps soy sauce   ☐ Salt and pepper

1. Cut the beef into very thin slices.

2. Heat the oil in a wok, add the meat and the ginger and stir-fry for
1 minute.

3. Pour off any excess fat, and stir in the tomato. Reduce the heat and
add the sugar, vinegar and the soy sauce.

4. Cook for a few minutes to allow the flavors to develop, then season
with salt and pepper to taste and serve immediately.

☐ TIME   Preparation takes about 10 minutes and cooking takes
approximately 5 minutes.

☐ SERVING IDEA   Serve with tomatoes, lightly seasoned with salt
and pepper and heated through in a steamer.

☐ CHECKPOINT   Do not allow the ginger to cook for too long, or
its flavor will be spoiled.

☐

OPPOSITE

**BEEF WITH
GINGER SAUCE**

STIR-FRIED LAMB WITH SESAME SEEDS

Lightly caramelized lamb, served on a bed of sautéed onions with a sesame seed flavored sauce.

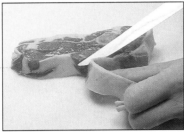

Step 1

Step 1

□ 2 tbsps oil □ 1lb 6oz shoulder of lamb, boned □ 2 onions, thinly sliced □ ½ clove garlic, chopped □ ½ cup lamb stock or other meat stock □ 1 tsp sugar □ 1 tbsp soy sauce □ ½ tsp wine vinegar □ Salt and pepper □ 1 tbsp sesame seeds

1. Cut away any excess fat from the lamb. Slice the meat very thinly, using a sharp knife. Heat the oil in a wok and stir-fry the lamb. Remove when cooked and set aside.

2. In the same oil, fry the onions and garlic. Once they have become transparent, remove them and set aside.

3. Pour off any excess fat and put the meat back in the wok with the lamb stock, sugar, soy sauce and vinegar. Continue cooking until the sauce is reduced. Season to taste with salt and pepper.

4. When the meat is lightly caramelized, sprinkle over the sesame seeds and stir. Serve hot on a bed of the sautéed onions.

□ TIME   Preparation takes about 10 minutes and cooking takes approximately 20 minutes.

□ VARIATION   Use any cut of lamb, cutting away any excess fat, before slicing very thinly.

□ CHECKPOINT   This recipe is served without sauce. As the meat is caramelized, it should stay moist.

□

OPPOSITE

STIR-FRIED
LAMB WITH
SESAME SEEDS

SERVES 4

LAMBS' KIDNEYS WITH ASPARAGUS

*Gently fried lambs' kidneys cooked in a sweet, spicy sauce
and served with asparagus tips.*

□ 12 green asparagus stalks   □ 4 lambs' kidneys   □ Salt and pepper
□ 4oz small dried black Chinese mushrooms, soaked for 15 minutes in
warm water   □ 2 tbsps oil   □ 1 shallot, chopped   □ 1 tsp dark soy
sauce   □ 1 tbsp hoisin sauce   □ 1 cup chicken stock   □ Few drops
chili sauce

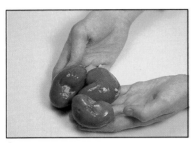

Step 2

Step 2

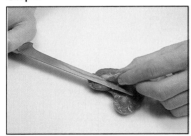

Step 2

1. Peel and trim the asparagus stalks and cook in boiling, lightly salted water until tender. Rinse in cold water and set aside to drain.

2. Buy kidneys which are of about the same size so that they cook evenly throughout. Cut the kidneys in half, cutting out any nerves and gristle. Season with salt and pepper.

3. Cook the mushrooms for about 10 minutes in a small quantity of boiling water. Rinse them in cold water and set aside to drain.

4. Heat the oil in a wok and cook the kidneys for approximately 3 minutes. Remove them and place on a kitchen towel or paper towels so that the blood is absorbed.

5. Pour off any excess fat from the wok and add the shallot, soy sauce, hoisin sauce, mushrooms, stock and chili sauce. Cook for 2 minutes.

6. Return the kidneys to the wok and cook until the sauce is slightly reduced.

7. Adjust the seasoning, adding salt and pepper to taste.

8. Reheat the asparagus by steaming lightly. Serve hot, with the kidneys in their sauce.

□ TIME   Preparation takes about 10 minutes and cooking takes approximately 35 minutes.

□ VARIATION   Green asparagus is usually the first to come in season, followed by the white variety. Use whichever is available.

□ CHECKPOINT   It is very important to leave the kidneys to drain completely on a kitchen towel or paper towels. They contain a lot of blood which might otherwise run during cooking (Step 6) and ruin the flavor of the dish.

□

OPPOSITE

LAMBS' KIDNEYS
WITH
ASPARAGUS

—— SERVES 4 ——

LAMB WITH TRANSPARENT NOODLES

*Quick-fried lamb, coated in a light, soy-based sauce and
served with transparent noodles.*

Step 4

Step 5

Step 6

☐ 1lb lean lamb   ☐ 4oz transparent noodles   ☐ 2 tbsps oil
☐ 1 tsp chopped garlic   ☐ 1 scallion, chopped   ☐ 2 tbsps soy sauce
☐ 1 cup lamb stock   ☐ Salt and pepper

1. Cut the meat into thin slices.

2. Bring a large quantity of salted water to the boil. Add the noodles and cook them for approximately 45 seconds. Rinse immediately in cold water and set aside to drain.

3. Heat the oil in a wok and stir-fry the garlic and scallion.

4. Add the meat slices to the wok and stir-fry for 1 minute.

5. Stir in the soy sauce and the stock and cook over a gentle heat until the meat is cooked through.

6. Add the well-drained noodles and allow to heat through. Adjust the seasoning, adding salt and pepper as necessary. Serve hot.

☐ TIME   Preparation takes about 10 minutes and cooking takes approximately 15 minutes.

☐ CHECKPOINT   Once the stock has been added to the wok, reduce the heat and finish cooking very slowly so that the stock does not evaporate.

☐ SERVING IDEA   Serve with steamed snow peas.

☐

OPPOSITE

LAMB WITH
TRANSPARENT
NOODLES

---- SERVES 4 ----

SAUTÉED FRUIT SALAD

*In this unusual fruit salad, the exotic ingredients are stir-fried
in a little oil and delicately flavored with cinnamon.*

Step 1

Step 2

□ 4 slices fresh pineapple   □ 4 jackfruit or breadfruit   □ 6 palm fruit
□ 1 grapefruit   □ 1 pear   □ ½ mango   □ 12 litchis, peeled
□ 2 tbsps oil   □ 2 tbsps sugar   □ Powdered cinnamon

1. Cut the pineapple, jackfruit or breadfruit and palm fruit into thin
slices. Peel the grapefruit and cut into segments. Peel the pear and the
mango, and cut both into thin slices.

2. Heat the oil and stir-fry the fruit in the following order: pineapple,
litchis, jackfruit or breadfruit, mango, pears, palm fruit and lastly the
grapefruit. Sprinkle with the sugar. Cook for a few more minutes and
sprinkle with the cinnamon.

3. Serve either hot or cold.

□   TIME   Preparation takes about 30 minutes and cooking takes
approximately 10 minutes.

□   VARIATION   Add a few strawberries once all the fruit is cooked.

□   COOK'S TIP   Vary the mixture of fruit according to season and
availability, but always stir-fry the most fragile fruit last, to retain its
shape and texture.

□

OPPOSITE

SAUTÉED FRUIT
SALAD

—— SERVES 4 ——

KUMQUATS WITH CANDIED GINGER

*If you serve this dessert to guests with a sweet tooth,
you just cannot go wrong!*

Step 1

Step 2

☐ 20 kumquats   ☐ 1-inch piece fresh ginger root, peeled and sliced
☐ 1 cup sugar

1. Using a brush, clean the kumquats. Blanch them in boiling water and drain. Blanch the ginger root slices in boiling water and drain in turn.

2. Place the blanched kumquats in a saucepan with the sugar. Cover with water to a height of 2 inches above the fruit. Add the sliced ginger and bring to the boil.

3. Reduce the heat and allow the liquid to reduce and caramelize gently. This is a long process, taking about 1½ hours. Add a little more water during cooking, if necessary.

4. Allow the dish to cool after cooking and then chill in the refrigerator. Cut the ginger into very small pieces before serving.

☐ TIME   Preparation takes about 20 minutes and cooking takes approximately 2 hours.

☐ SERVING IDEA   Cook the two ingredients separately, in case one of your guests does not like the flavor of one of them.

☐ CHECKPOINT   The cooking should be done very slowly, so that the sugar penetrates to the very center of the kumquats.

☐

OPPOSITE

KUMQUATS WITH
CANDIED GINGER

— SERVES 4 —

RICE PUDDINGS WITH CANDIED FRUIT

These puddings have a very unusual flavor, a little strange to Western palates, but tasty nonetheless!

Step 5

Step 5

Step 5

☐ 2 cups glutinous rice   ☐ 4 tbsps sugar   ☐ ⅓ cup candied fruit, chopped   ☐ 2 drops bitter almond essence   ☐ 20 dates, pitted   ☐ 1 tsp oil, warmed

1. Rinse the rice first in cold then in hot water. Place in a saucepan and cover with water to a height of ½ inch above the top of the rice, bring to the boil and cook, stirring occasionally. Once the rice is almost cooked, remove the pan from the heat. The rice will finish cooking in the hot water by itself.

2. Stir in the sugar, candied fruit and almond essence. Set aside to cool.

3. Place the dates in a food processor and blend until a smooth, solid paste forms.

4. Using your fingers, work this paste into 4 flat, even circles to fit individual molds.

5. Grease 4 individual molds with the warmed oil and place a layer of rice in the bottom. Place a date circle on top and finish with another layer of rice.

6. Cook the molds in a steamer for 30 minutes, to allow the flavors to mix and develop. Allow to cool and then chill in the refrigerator before serving.

☐ TIME   Preparation takes about 45 minutes and cooking takes 30 minutes. Cooking the glutinous rice takes about 20 minutes.

☐ VARIATION   Cook the rice in milk instead of water. Add a little chopped candied ginger to the rice mixture.

☐

OPPOSITE

RICE PUDDINGS WITH CANDIED FRUIT

MELON SALAD

*A refreshing fruit salad, which is especially tasty served after
a heavy meal of many courses.*

Step 1

Step 1

☐ 1 large cantaloupe melon   ☐ 1 mango   ☐ 4 canned litchis
☐ 4 large or 8 small strawberries   ☐ Litchi syrup from the can

1. Peel and seed the melon and cut into thin slices.

2. Peel and pit the mango and cut into thin slices.

3. Using a melon baller, cut as many balls as possible out of the strawberries.

4. Arrange the melon slices evenly on 4 small plates.

5. Spread a layer of mango over the melon. Place a litchi in the center of each plate and arrange a few strawberry balls around the edges.

6. Divide the litchi syrup evenly between the plates of fruit and chill them in the refrigerator before serving.

☐   TIME   Preparation takes about 30 minutes.

☐   VARIATION   Use a honeydew melon instead of the cantaloupe variety.

☐   COOK'S TIP   This dessert is best served well chilled from the refrigerator, so prepare it several hours in advance of serving.

☐

OPPOSITE

MELON SALAD

————— SERVES 4 —————

STUFFED LITCHIS

Mouthwatering litchis, stuffed with a mixture of dates and bananas.

Step 2

Step 3

Step 3

☐ 10 dates, pitted   ☐ 2 bananas   ☐ Juice of ½ lemon   ☐ 20 canned litchis, reserving a little syrup for the sauce

1. Place the pitted dates in a food processor and blend until a thick paste forms.

2. Peel and mash the bananas with the lemon juice. Add the date paste and mix together well.

3. Place the mixture in a pastry bag and use to stuff the litchis.

4. Mix the litchi syrup into the leftover stuffing to make a sauce. Serve the stuffed, chilled litchis with the sauce.

☐ TIME   Preparation takes about 30 minutes.

☐ VARIATION   You could use fresh litchis, which should be pitted before stuffing. Make a syrup with equal parts of water and sugar lightly boiled together, to replace the litchi syrup from the can.

☐ CHECKPOINT   The lemon is a very necessary addition to prevent the bananas turning black.

☐

OPPOSITE

STUFFED LITCHIS

—— SERVES 4 ——

DATE DUMPLINGS

*Light and puffy, these steamed date dumplings are
delicious served with a raspberry sauce.*

Step 1

Step 2

Step 2

☐ ½ cup water   ☐ ½ cup milk   ☐ 2 tsps baking powder
☐ 1 tbsp sugar   ☐ 1 pinch salt   ☐ 3½ cups all-purpose flour, sifted
☐ 15 dates, pitted   ☐ 1 tbsp ground almonds

1. Mix together the water and the milk. Incorporate the baking powder, sugar and salt.

2. Stirring well, incorporate the flour gradually into the above mixture, forming it into a ball. You may find it easier to use your fingers, rather than a spoon.

3. Let the dough rest in a warm place for 1 hour.

4. Place the dates and the almonds in a food processor and blend until a smooth paste is formed.

5. On a lightly floured surface, roll out small lumps of the dough into circles.

6. Place a little of the date mixture in the center of each circle. Pull the edges up over the top, pinching them together well with your fingers to seal. Roll in your hands to form small balls.

7. Steam the dumplings for approximately 20 minutes. You may need to do this in more than one batch.

8. Serve hot or cold.

☐ TIME   Preparation takes about 1 hour 20 minutes and cooking takes approximately 20 minutes per batch.

☐ SERVING IDEA   Serve the dumplings with a raspberry sauce. Crush fresh raspberries and add sifted icing sugar to taste. Mix together well and serve.

☐ CHECKPOINT   Make sure that you pinch the edges of the dumplings together firmly with your fingers before rolling them into balls.

☐

OPPOSITE

DATE
DUMPLINGS

SERVES 4

HALF-MOON BANANA PASTRIES

*These crunchy pastries are rather dry, and are traditionally
served with a cup of Chinese tea.*

Step 1

Step 1

PASTRY DOUGH

☐ 4 cups all-purpose flour, sifted   ☐ ½ cup shortening   ☐ Pinch salt
☐ ½ cup water

FILLING

☐ 3 bananas   ☐ 2 tsps sugar   ☐ Pinch cinnamon   ☐ Few drops of
lemon juice   ☐ 1 egg yolk, beaten

1. Cut the shortening into the flour with the salt. Using your fingers, incorporate the water gradually to form a ball. Wrap a damp cloth around the dough and leave it to rest in a cool place for 30 minutes.

2. Peel and crush the bananas with a fork. Add the sugar, cinnamon and lemon juice. Mix together well.

3. Roll out small pieces of dough on a lightly floured surface, and cut into circles. Place a little of the banana filling on each round of dough. Fold into half-moon shapes and seal the edges first by pinching together with your fingers and then by decorating with a fork.

4. Continue until all the dough and filling have been used.

5. Brush the beaten egg yolk over the half-moon pastries. Pierce the pastries once to allow steam to escape during cooking. Cook in a moderate oven, 350°F, for approximately 20 minutes, until crisp and golden.

☐ TIME   Preparation takes about 25 minutes, resting time for the dough is 30 minutes and cooking takes approximately 20 minutes.

☐ VARIATION   Make up the pastries using different fruit fillings.

☐ COOK'S TIP   The cooked dough in this recipe is very crisp. Serve the pastries with a fruit drink in summer and hot Chinese tea in winter.

☐ CHECKPOINT   Be sure to seal the edges of the pastries thoroughly so that no filling escapes during cooking.

☐

OPPOSITE

HALF-MOON BANANA PASTRIES

———— SERVES 4 ————

ALMOND JELLY

*A smooth almond jelly, which is very tasty served with
fresh litchis or half-moon pastries.*

Step 2

Step 2

Step 3

□ 1¼ cups milk   □ 3 sheets gelatin, pre-soaked in cold water,
or1 package powdered gelatin, soaked in 1 tbsp water
□ ⅛ cup powdered almonds   □ 5 drops almond extract
□ ¼ cup sugar   □ 1 can litchis

1. Heat the milk in a saucepan until hot, but not boiling.

2. Drain the pre-soaked gelatin sheets very carefully, if using. They should not drip water during the next step. Stir the gelatin into the hot milk.

3. Stir in the powdered almonds, almond extract and sugar.

4. Stir well, until the gelatin has dissolved. Using a wire whisk will make the job easier.

5. Pour the liquid jelly into a soup plate and leave in the refrigerator for at least 2 hours until set.

6. Once the jelly has set, turn it out onto a cutting board and cut into slices, or any other shapes.

7. Place the slices on a serving plate, decorate with the litchis and pour over a little of the juice from the tin.

□ TIME   Preparation takes about 1 hour and it takes at least 2 hours for the jelly to set.

□ CHECKPOINT   If you have trouble removing the jelly from the soup plate, cut it into slices whilst still in the plate. Remove a few of the slices and give the plate a good shake. The remaining jelly should then come loose.

□

OPPOSITE

ALMOND JELLY

---- SERVES 4 ----

RICE IN MILK

This is delicious served either hot or cold.

Step 3

Step 4

□ ½ cup long grain rice   □ 2½ cups milk   □ 1 tbsp clear honey
□ ¼ tsp powdered cinnamon   □ 5 cubes sugar

---

1. Blanch the rice in boiling water, rinse well and set aside to drain.

2. Pour the milk into a saucepan and stir in the honey.

3. Sprinkle in the cinnamon.

4. Stir in the well-drained rice and the sugar cubes. Cook over a gentle heat, stirring from time to time.

5. Once the rice has absorbed all the liquid, remove from the heat.

6. Serve either hot or cold.

□ TIME   Preparation takes about 10 minutes and cooking takes approximately 20 minutes, but can vary according to the quality of the rice. Remove from the heat as soon as all the liquid has been absorbed.

□ SERVING IDEA   Allow the rice to cool before chilling in the refrigerator. Scoop out balls of the chilled rice with an ice cream scoop and serve with a fresh raspberry coulis.

□ VARIATION   The rice can be cooked in the oven in a covered casserole. If so, it is very important to monitor the level of the liquid, and to remove the casserole as soon as the rice has absorbed all the liquid.

□

OPPOSITE

RICE IN MILK

————— SERVES 4 —————

KIWI AND COCONUT DUO

*Incredibly simple to prepare, this recipe is a delicious blend of kiwi
fruit, fresh coconut and coconut milk.*

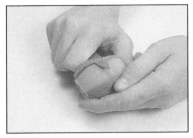

Step 2

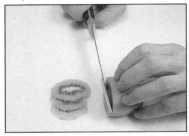

Step 3

□ 4 kiwi fruit   □ 1 fresh coconut   □ A little sugar (optional)

1. Remove the stalks from the ends of the kiwis.

2. Peel them lengthwise with a small sharp knife.

3. Slice them thinly widthways.

4. Cut the coconut into pieces, reserving all the milk.

5. Cut the coconut flesh into very thin slices.

6. Arrange the kiwi slices on a serving plate and surround with the slices of coconut.

7. Add a little sugar to the coconut milk if desired and pour over the fruit. Serve chilled.

□ TIME   Preparation takes about 25 minutes.

□ VARIATION   Coconut milk can now be bought in cans. It is usually of very high quality and is thicker than fresh coconut milk.

□ COOK'S TIP   The addition of sugar to the milk is optional, and depends upon the acidity of the milk.

□

OPPOSITE

**KIWI AND
COCONUT DUO**

--- SERVES 4 ---

PEANUT BUTTER CAKE

*This peanut butter cake is light but nonetheless quite filling
and is very good served chilled.*

Step 1

Step 2

Step 4

Step 5

□ ½ cup margarine, softened to room temperature   □ ¼ cup sugar
□ 4 eggs, separated and the whites stiffly whipped   □ 1 cup all-
purpose flour, sifted   □ Pinch salt   □ 2 tbsps smooth peanut butter
□ 1 tsp vanilla sugar, or ½ tsp vanilla extract + 1 tsp sugar
□ 1 tsp grated lemon peel

---

1. Beat or whip together the softened margarine and the sugar until light and fluffy.

2. Add the egg yolks and beat them in well.

3. Beat in the sifted flour and the salt.

4. Add the peanut butter, vanilla sugar and the lemon peel. Beat well to combine all the ingredients.

5. Using a metal spoon or rubber spatula, gently incorporate half the egg whites into the mixture.

6. Gently incorporate the remaining egg whites. Pour the cake mixture into a nonstick baking pan and cook in a moderate oven, 350°F, until the cake has risen slightly and is firm to the touch.

7. Allow to cool, before removing from the pan. Serve either slightly warm or chilled.

□   TIME   Preparation takes about 15 minutes and cooking takes approximately 30 minutes.

□   SERVING IDEA   Cut the cake into decorative shapes using a sharp knife or biscuit cutter and serve with a kiwi coulis, sweetened to taste with a little sugar.

□   CHECKPOINT   Incorporate the egg whites as described. If they are whipped in, the mixture will fall.

□

OPPOSITE

PEANUT BUTTER
CAKE

——— SERVES 4 ———

EXOTIC FRUIT SALAD

Fresh fruit marinated in orange and litchi juice with just a hint of almond.

Step 1

Step 1

Step 1

☐ 1 papaya ☐ 1 pomegranate ☐ 2 kiwi fruit ☐ 4 rambutan fruit ☐ 4 canned litchis, plus the juice from the can ☐ 3 blood oranges ☐ 3 drops bitter almond extract, or ordinary almond extract

1. Peel all the fruit except the oranges, removing pips or pitting each fruit as necessary. Try to buy a fully ripe papaya for the salad. Cut it in half. Using a small spoon, remove all the pips and any stringy skin around them. Peel each half, but not too thickly as the flesh immediately below the skin is very good. Finally, cut the flesh into thin slices or other fancy shapes.

2. Peel two of the oranges. Remove all the pith and cut the flesh into small pieces.

3. Squeeze the juice from the remaining orange, mix this with the canned litchi juice and add the almond extract.

4. Cut all the remaining fruit into slices, rounds or small cubes and combine these with the prepared papaya and oranges in a bowl. Pour over the almondflavored juices and leave the salad to marinate for a few hours in the refrigerator.

5. Serve chilled.

☐ TIME   Preparation takes about 1 hour and the salad should be left to marinate for at least 3 hours.

☐ SERVING IDEA   Cut a few fresh mint leaves into thin strips to garnish the fruit salad just before serving.

☐ CHECKPOINT   Exotic fruit often arrives in the shops before it is ripe. The solution is to sweeten the sauce slightly before marinating the fruit in order to eliminate acidity.

☐ BUYING GUIDE   If any of the fruits are out of season and unavailable, substitute other appropriate fruit, as desired.

☐

OPPOSITE

EXOTIC FRUIT SALAD